Jacques Coeur

Jacques Coeur. Wood Engraving by Grignon (1653) after Anonymous Portrait, 15th c. (Stock Montage, Inc.)

Kathryn L. Reyerson

University of Minnesota

Jacques Coeur

Entrepreneur and King's Bursar

The Library of World Biography

Series Editor: Peter N. Stearns

New York   San Francisco   Boston
London   Toronto   Sydney   Tokyo   Singapore   Madrid
Mexico City   Munich   Paris   Cape Town   Hong Kong   Montreal

Vice President and Publisher: Priscilla McGeehon
Acquisitions Editor: Erika Gutierrez
Executive Marketing Manager: Sue Westmoreland
Production Coordinator: Shafiena Ghani
Senior Cover Design Manager/Designer: Nancy Danahy
Manufacturing Buyer: Roy L. Pickering
Electronic Page Makeup: Jeff Henn
Printer and Binder: R R Donnelley and Sons Company / Harrisonburg
Cover Printer: Coral Graphics, Inc.

All photos are the property of the author except where noted.

Library of Congress Cataloging-in-Publication Data

Reyerson, Kathryn
    Jacques Coeur: entrepreneur and king's bursar /
        Kathryn L. Reyerson;
        p. cm.—(Library of world biography)
    Includes bibliographical references and index.
    ISBN 0-321-08537-X
        1. Coeur, Jacques D. 1456.   2. Capitalists and financiers—
    France—Biography.   3. France—History—Charles VII,
    1422–1461   I. Title.   II. Series.

    HJ1077.C6R49.2004
    381'.092—dc22
    [B]   2004046482

Please visit our website at http://www.ablongman.com

ISBN 0-321-08537-X

1 2 3 4 5 6 7 8 9 10—DOH—07 06 05 04

To my sons James Dil (Jacques Coeur) and Philip Rajan

Contents

Editor's Preface

"Biography is history seen through the prism of a person."
—LOUIS FISCHER

It is often challenging to identify the roles and experiences of individuals in world history. Larger forces predominate. Yet biography provides important access to world history. It shows how individuals helped shape the society around them. Biography also offers concrete illustrations of larger patterns, in political and intellectual life, in family, and in the economy.

The Longman Library of World Biography series seeks to capture the individuality and drama that mark human character. But it also deals with individuals operating in one of the main world history periods, while also reflecting issues in the particular society around them. Here, the individual illustrates larger themes of time and place. The interplay between the personal and the general is always the key to using biography in history, and world history is no exception. Always too, there is the question of personal agency: how much do individuals, even great ones, shape their own lives and environment, and how much are they shaped by the world around them?

PETER N. STEARNS

Author's Preface

Jacques Coeur was both a successful business entrepreneur and a royal official, a bursar charged with provisioning the royal household in luxury goods of all kinds. He was called *argentier*, in fact, the "*argentier du roi.*" His career was the stuff of legend. He rose very high within French society, and when he fell from power and royal favor, it was with disgrace and accusations of treason and mismanagement of funds. He led France into the forefront of Mediterranean commercial exploits in the Near East, an unaccustomed arena for the French. Condemned in 1453, the year to which most medievalists assign the end of the Middle Ages because it witnessed the conclusion of the Hundred Years War and the fall of Constantinople to the Turks, Jacques Coeur died in 1456 on the eastern Mediterranean island of Chios on a papal crusade against the Turks.

I came to the study of Coeur after many years of focus on the southern French town of Montpellier that was a site of Coeur's Mediterranean operations. In Montpellier there is even a street named after him. The career of Jacques Coeur provides the historian with a broad canvas on which to explore many historical problems. The end of the Hundred Years War meant victory for France over England but also the maturing of institutions of government, permanent taxation, and a standing army. After a hundred plus years of crisis during which France was the battlefield, and factionalism was rife (Armagnacs and Burgundians), the monarchy in the person of Charles VII also emerged victorious. France could now resume a role on a European stage. Jacques Coeur played a pivotal role in French victory and in the institutional evolution in this era of transition.

The story of Jacques Coeur has the drama and passion to retain the interest of readers. He was shipwrecked and captured by pirates. He was ennobled and joined the king's council. He was a friend of kings and popes. He inspired loyalty in his friends, and they would be tested. He was accused of poisoning the king's mistress, Agnès Sorel, and of the provisioning of the Saracens ("our ancient enemies of the Christian faith") in materiel of war. Court intrigue, tremendous ego, and unorthodox entrepreneurship underpinned the downfall of Coeur.

Coeur was a new man in the fifteenth century, a commoner in origin who became almost as wealthy as the king. His career is a harbinger for developments in early modern French officialdom. Through the lense of Jacques Coeur's life, readers will be exposed to the spheres of economy and politics in France and northern Europe, and through Coeur's Mediterranean policies and his fleet of ships, to the wider world. His role in championing French maritime trade foreshadowed later French mercantilist exploits.

Appearing in a very diverse world history biography series with Longman, this study will be a vehicle for familiarizing readers with Europe and the Mediterranean of the mid-fifteenth century as it examines Jacques Coeur on several levels: on a French stage, within the mercantile and royal milieux of late medieval France at the end of the Hundred Years War; on a Mediterranean stage which had been the traditional domain of southern European merchants; and finally, on a world history stage within a broader comparative context at the beginning of the period of European expansion in the age of exploration.

An extensive glossary and an explanatory note on medieval money at the end of this volume will assist readers unfamiliar with the Middle Ages. The "Note on the Sources" that describes in detail my reading and research in preparing this project can be used as a guide to further reading. Jacques Coeur has been the focus of many books in European, particularly French, scholarship. Evidence regarding Coeur is scattered in archives across France and beyond. The historian Michel Mollat edited a particularly valuable source, the journal of the high court prosecutor, Jean Dauvet, who was charged by the king with the confiscation of Coeur's fortune after his condemnation. Writers contemporary with the fifteenth-century Coeur wrote about him, providing very useful commentary on his contributions and his persona.

I traveled twice to Bourges to photograph the magnificent house that Coeur built at the end of his career. It is a remarkable structure, worthy of the term "palace." Visual evidence from the house and its decor, along with descriptions of the lovely town of Bourges, offer readers insights into Coeur, the man.

There are considerable differences of opinion among scholars about how to interpret Coeur. I provide arguments for my own assessment of Coeur as a multifaceted figure, king's officer, merchant and entrepreneur, financier, with an intermingling of public and private roles that was consistent with medieval practice. I trust my readers will agree that Coeur is, in fact, worthy of his motto, "For the valiant of heart, nothing is impossible."

Thanks are due first and foremost to my friend Marguerite Ragnow, Associate Director of the Center for Early Modern History at the University of Minnesota, for her invaluable suggestions for this book. I am also grateful to the many audiences who listened to me talk about Jacques Coeur: in France in the seminar of Claude Gauvard and Robert Jacob of the Université de Paris I - La Sorbonne and that of Elisabeth Crouzet Pavan of the Université de Paris IV - La Sorbonne; at the University of Minnesota in the Medieval Research Group; at the Western Society for French History in Los Angeles; at the International Congress on Medieval Studies, The Medieval Institute, Western Michigan University in Kalamazoo; and at the Ecole Française de Rome. Thanks also to Peter Stearns, to Alfred Soman, Erika Gutierrez of Longman Publishers, and to the many reviewers: Fred Burkhard, Eric Dursteler, Dean T. Ferguson, Margaret Sankey, Robert J. Caputi, Dr. Lloyd Johnson, Dr. L. Edward Hicks, Dr. Travis H. Ricketts, Gary Lester, Kathleen S. Carter, Kenneth Faunce, Joanne Klein, Jan Maxwell, Roger Schlesinger, Denise Williams, Mary Lauranne Lifka, Sally Eads, and Dave A. Shaker. Any remaining errors are my responsibility alone.

I wish to acknowledge the assistance of the staffs of the Bibliothèque des Quatre Piliers in Bourges, the Archives Départementales de l'Hérault in Montpellier, the Bibliothèque Municipale de Montpellier, and the Palais de Jacques Coeur in Bourges.

The research and writing for this study were made possible through a single-semester leave from the University of Minnesota and by funding from a McKnight Research Fellowship, a University of Minnesota/McKnight Summer Research Fellowship, the McMillan Travel funds, the Office of International Programs, and the Office of the Provost and Vice President for Academic Affairs of the University of Minnesota.

KATHRYN L. REYERSON

Jacques Coeur

Introduction

If an opinion survey such as the Gallup Poll had questioned a fifteenth-century audience to determine the richest and most powerful man in France in the 1440s, it is highly likely the answer would have been Jacques Coeur. Coeur held the post of royal bursar, a supply officer with the responsibility of catering to the needs of the royal household, primarily in luxury goods, but he was also a very successful businessman, an international financier, and a Mediterranean merchant. The French term for Coeur was *argentier*. The *Argenterie* operated as a royal commissary with a particularly posh line of products. Mention "the" *argentier* to a fifteenth-century Frenchman and his immediate identification would have been Jacques Coeur. As *argentier* of the king (*"argentier du roi"*), Coeur's renown spread throughout Europe.

Coeur rose very high within the social hierarchy in France, and he and his family were ennobled by the king in recompense for remarkable service. Coeur created a central and northern French presence in trade in the Mediterranean and the Near East, an unaccustomed role, although the southern French had been involved commercially in these areas for centuries. In keeping with a pattern for certain celebrated French royal officials before and after him, Coeur ultimately fell from power and royal favor. He was arrested on 31 July 1451, disgraced and accused of several instances of treason, monetary fraud, mismanagement of funds, and tax extortion. He was also suspected of poisoning Agnès Sorel, the king's mistress, and of provisioning Saracens with materiel of war. Court intrigue contributed to his downfall. King Charles VII (1422–1461) issued an order (*arrêt de condamnation*) on 29 May 1453, sentencing Coeur to death, commuted to permanent banishment after the confiscation of his goods to pay 100,000 *écus* in debts to the king and 300,000 *écus* in fines. Coeur escaped his prison in late 1454 and fled France for exile under papal protection in Rome, only to die in 1456 on the island of Chios during a papal crusade to the eastern Mediterranean.

After the death of Jacques Coeur, his life and actions quickly became a subject for fifteenth-century writers, his contemporaries, and immediate followers. Few figures in the Middle Ages achieved such a level of popular renown for better or worse. Among others, chroniclers Thomas Basin, Mathieu d'Escouchy, Georges Chastellain, and even the Parisian underworld poet and great lyricist François Villon made reference to his fate. They were intrigued and fascinated by the man. Villon evoked Coeur in his *Testament*:

> Lamenting my poverty
> Often my heart tells me
> Man do not be so sad
> Nor dwell in such despair,
> If you have not as much as Jacques Coeur.
> Better to live without great display,
> Poor, than to have been a lord
> And rot under rich tombs.[1]

Death as the great equalizer caused even the wealthy to molder in their tombs, and their fate was perhaps worse, given how far they had fallen.

The opinions of writers of the reign of Louis XI (1461–1483) recalled the classic accusations against Coeur but also the envy of his contemporaries and their desire to get their hands on his wealth. A little later, Claude de Seyssel, an officer and legal authority of Louis XII (1498–1515), was explicit in stating that Coeur, one of the wisest and wealthiest men of the kingdom of Charles VII, was persecuted by the king, though Coeur more than any other had helped Charles recover his realm and drive out his enemies "the English".[2] According to Seyssel, Charles VII did this out of suspicion that Coeur poisoned his mistress Agnès. Seyssel judged the other crimes of which Coeur was accused insufficient to justify the severity of punishment. The vision of contemporary and near contemporary

---

[1] Villon, 18–19; Clément, I: XXIX.

[2] Clément, II–XXXI.

writers was almost uniformly in favor of Coeur and against the condemnation he had received at the hands of Charles VII.

French scholarship in the intervening centuries has not forgotten Coeur. In 1853 historian Pierre Clément wrote an important study, *Jacques Coeur et Charles VII*, providing useful source material of various kinds, including quotations about Coeur by fifteenth-century authors. Modern French historians have debated whether to categorize Jacques Coeur as royal official, financier, or merchant. They have constructed radically differing interpretations of Coeur. The distinguished twentieth-century economic, social, and maritime historian Michel Mollat saw Coeur as a merchant and entrepreneur first and foremost. For economic historian Jacques Heers, he was primarily a royal official and a statesman, only secondarily a merchant, and a palace merchant at that, not an independent operator. Heers questioned how profitable Coeur's Mediterranean trade actually was. Coeur's own fifteenth century saw him as a hybrid, part merchant, part official, and found no contradictions in that dichotomy. There is much to be said for the fifteenth-century assessment of the man.

There have been few treatments of Coeur in English. In spite of the somewhat dated, but nonetheless interesting 1927 study, *Jacques Coeur. Merchant Prince of the Middle Ages*, by Albert Boardman Kerr, he is not well known to an English-language audience. It is time for a new assessment in English of the life of Coeur. However, for a period as far removed as the late Middle Ages, answers to the kinds of questions that twentieth- and twenty-first century biographies raise are often unavailable. Jacques Coeur made no comments on his personal belief system. There remains no diary of his daily life. He left little by way of letters aside from a very modest set of documents dealing primarily with business matters. Exceptions of a more personal and emotional nature would be his words of reassurance to his wife, Macée, in late July 1451, just before his arrest, and a plea for help to a relative and close collaborator, Jean de Village, during his escape. Absent in Coeur's case is the voluminous correspondence preserved for a few late medieval figures such as the Italian merchant Francesco Datini of Prato (ca. 1335–1410).

The figure cut by the *argentier* is of interest to readers. Because of Coeur's historical significance, paintings purportedly depicting him were produced over the centuries, but, unfortunately, there is no verifiable contemporary representation of the man, and his real likeness is unknown.[3] Kerr noted the presence among debtors of Coeur of celebrated painters of the time: Jacob de Litemont and Jean Fouquet. Piero della Francesca may have painted him, but no such painting has survived.[4] Kerr assembled several descriptions of Coeur's appearance from comments made during the time his supporters were trying to get him declared an ecclesiastic and thus subject to lesser forms of punishment during his trial. At issue was whether Coeur was tonsured (the shaved head of clergymen). Several witnesses described seeing him without a beard but not tonsured. In the course of their testimony they also offered other commentary. A certain André Vidal remarked:

> With regard to his habit, I have seen him in the past wear one without a collar, the sleeves of the doublet being striped with red against a black background. During his visit to Normandy, I have seen him wear a hat covered with velvet with large silk folds on top; long-pointed laced shoes. I have also seen him wear generally a short robe, reaching halfway to the knees, gathered at the shoulders and open at the sleeves, red or green-and-gray shoes, and robes of all colors, several of them being without a collar, in the style that gentlemen of the court are wont to attire themselves.[5]

Another observer, Aubert Panois, described a further image of Coeur, suggesting that the *argentier* cut a stylish figure among his contemporaries:

> I have seen Jacques Coeur wear a large hat of scarlet brocade and a robe without a collar, reaching halfway to his knees,

---

[3] Among the paintings, a miniature of Jean Colombe in the Münchner Stundenbuch of the Bayrische Staatsbibliothek in Munich, perhaps depicting Jacques Coeur in prayer; Jacques Coeur performing *amende honorable* before the king in a miniature of the Chronicle of Monstrelet; a nineteenth-century painting by J. Boilly in *I Benefattori dell'Umanità* (Florence, 1860); a 1653 engraved plate of Grignon in the French historian Denis Godefroy's *Histoire de Charles VII*, after a fifteenth-century anonymous painting (the frontispiec of this book). Other illustrations of Coeur include the miniature of Dunois, Brézé, and Coeur at the entry of Charles VII into Rouen from the *Vigiles de Charles VII* by Martial d'Auvergne (Bibliothèque Nationale, ms. fr. 5054, f. 182v). The statue on the cover and spine of this book stands in front of Jacques Coeur's house in Bourges.

[4] Kerr, 130.

[5] Kerr, 131.

gathered at the sleeves, heavily bordered with sable and slashed at the sides. This was in 1447, 1448, and the years following. I have never seen Jacques Coeur wear a long robe except during the past year, two months before his arrest, in the month of May, 1451. Then I saw him wear, at Montpellier, a long robe, I do not recall of what color, trimmed with vair; I have seen him wear hose of scarlet and other colors and long-pointed laced shoes. Whether at the time two months before his arrest or always when I have seen him, he was dressed like a layman. More I do not know.[6]

Given that he featured furs and cloths of many colors at the stores of the *Argenterie*, Coeur appears to have been a good client of his own operation. He fancied lavish but tasteful attire.

Legal records regarding Coeur are the best preserved. During his treason trial near the end of his life, many witnesses were interrogated by the king's commissioners, and some of these testimonies survive. After Coeur's condemnation by the king, Jean Dauvet, a royal prosecutor of the Parisian high court (*procureur général au Parlement de Paris*), was sent to confiscate Coeur's fortune in order to repay the debts and fines owed the king. A highly competent and conscientious royal official, Dauvet left a lengthy journal account of his travels and experiences in the period of 1453–1457 in his efforts to identify Coeur's assets. Dauvet questioned many individuals—friends and enemies—about Jacques Coeur in his search for the sources of Coeur's wealth. Witnesses did not hesitate to comment broadly about Coeur. Supporters may have embroidered on the qualities and accomplishments of the man while enemies exaggerated his faults. Rehabilitation attempts by Coeur's sons after his death suffer from the same potential distortion, yet these documents are also useful in tracing Coeur's life. Handled with care, they can inform the historian about Jacques Coeur's life and actions, once the issue of bias has been addressed.

In addition to close scrutiny of modern scholarship and examination of primary sources, it is helpful to study the man in the context of his times. The fifteenth century was a transitional period between the Middle Ages and the early modern era. Historians often use the year 1453, the date of the end of the Hundred Years War and of the fall of Constantinople to the Turks, as the climax

---

[6] Kerr, 132. Vair is squirrel fur.

of the Middle Ages.[7] During the lengthy period of war, 1337–1453, France and England developed from medieval kingdoms into nascent early modern states with a sense of national identity, governmental institutions such as legislative bodies and central law courts, royal financial organs, and a strong monarchy. There was evolution, as well, in the areas of society and economy. Jacques Coeur was a transitional figure, medieval and traditional in some areas, innovative in others. Though hardly a typical fifteenth-century personage, Coeur can serve as a microcosm for the changes occurring in the fifteenth-century macrocosm. Larger than life, he was himself a force for change. This study will situate Coeur in his era in order to illuminate both the man and his time.

The Hundred Years War placed a tremendous financial burden on Charles VII, stemming from decades of a war economy. His main challenge was to field an army. At the opening of the war in 1337, France had neither a permanent army nor adequate regularly recurring financial support from taxation. In the 1440s Jacques Coeur contributed through his financial aid, monetary policies, and administrative innovation to the stabilization of royal finance that led to the creation of a standing army, a force of men always under arms, freeing the king from the need to assemble a military force at each crisis. A standing army sustained by permanent taxation was, arguably, the most significant institutional result of the Hundred Years War for France. At the end of the fifteenth-century the king of France could field a permanent army of 25,000 men. Coeur's financial contributions to the royal cause made it possible for Charles VII to win the Hundred Years War.

Coeur represents an early example of involvement of men in royal employ as lenders to the monarchy. From the early fourteenth century on, French kings relied less and less on financing by Italian merchant-bankers, preferring to find funding sources in their own kingdom. They broadcast their fiscal needs to a large audience of clergy and towns to finance the wars in Flanders and then the multiple campaigns of the Hundred Years War. Spread broadly, many loans to the king were modest, though in the case of Jacques Coeur, his loans to Charles VII were not. By the late fifteenth century Louis XI routinely

---

[7] Coeur's condemnation occurred on the very day of the fall of Constantinople, 29 May 1453.

included royal officers in this fiscal responsibility by means of loans that were often obligatory (forced) and without interest. The extraordinary level of indebtedness of Charles VII to Coeur undoubtedly played an important part in the latter's fall from grace. In the long run, the financial relations between the king and his officers, that is, royal indebtedness, led to the development in the *Ancien Régime* of the hereditary transmission of royal office and its **venality** (purchase).

On another front, Coeur broke the old mold of traditional French society in which nobility was conferred by birth or battlefield glory. He was a commoner who became a noble, a man whose wealth rivaled that of the king of France. In the late medieval and early modern periods royal service proved a more reliable source of wealth than did trade. Jacques Coeur exemplified the career trajectory of merchants who joined royal service, became ennobled, and finally established a landed fortune. Before his arrest in 1451 Coeur was deeply invested in this last phase of social ascension as land in the Middle Ages was the primary source of wealth and status. His newly acquired noble station fed his pride and encouraged a certain ostentation, but he had taste, evident in his still-extant home in Bourges, south of Paris in central France. Early on in his career he demonstrated a keen eye for luxury products with which to stock the *Argenterie*. His ambition outran his ability to pay his debts in timely fashion, and he had cash flow problems. He had business rivals who became his enemies. On balance, he was a self-made man, not overly cultured, with something of the nouveau-riche about him. Enjoying his wealth, he was a consumer of all the fifteenth century could offer in terms of luxury accommodations and amenities. Coeur was part of a group of royal officials of non-noble origin, partaking fully of the social and political transition of governance in late medieval France. His ennoblement and that of some of his contemporaries foreshadowed the emergence of the *noblesse de robe* (nobility of the robe, as opposed to the traditional nobility of the sword, *noblesse d'épée*), frequently the result of a legal career in royal service under the Ancien Régime. In Coeur's era, the vulnerability of such newly promoted commoners was patent. His success offended France's lingering medieval chivalric ways and may have incited the envy of the king himself.

If there are many reasons to consider Coeur a transitional figure in a time of change, on several levels his actions mirror those of a medieval man. His traditional religious enthusiasms are reflected in his support of the cathedral of Bourges, in his placement of two of his sons in church office, in his close association with popes, and in his participation in a crusade. With traditional attachment to his *pays*, his homeland in the Berry, and to his birthplace of Bourges, he built his commercial and financial empire with a close-knit team of associates. This tactic was indeed one of the secrets of his success. Many of his business techniques resembled those of the thirteenth century; his Mediterranean trade was not significantly different from that of Italians of an earlier era. His hands-on management was innovative, and his integration of economic activities and coordination of trade, transport, and marketing were very sophisticated for the fifteenth century.

In the context of world history Jacques Coeur was both traditional and forward-looking. He was not an explorer of new lands and thus did not participate in the maritime adventures that later led to the European "Age of Discoveries." However, his emphasis on French Mediterranean trade and his willingness to deal with Islamic rulers, albeit with some ambivalence, set the tone for future French moves on a world stage. Determined to create a role for France in the Mediterranean, Coeur arranged alliances with the sultan of Egypt to facilitate French trade in Alexandria. Equally avant-garde, foreshadowing later **mercantilism** (state-sponsored and state-regulated economic activity), was his construction of a French Mediterranean fleet with the king's financing. Louis XI, the bourgeois king, later built upon the economic daring of Jacques Coeur in his stimulus of the fairs of Lyon to rival those of Geneva and in his patronage of galleys sailing under the French royal flag in pursuit of Mediterranean trade. François I (1515–1547) promoted French Mediterranean trade and from 1525 made alliances with the Turks, even to the extent of the creation of a Franco-Turkish fleet. Coeur's actions on behalf of the royal economy provided a precedent for early modern mercantilism that led France to commercial adventures in North America and Asia.

Although a certain ambivalence about whether he was medieval or transitional persists in modern assessments of the man, Coeur never concerned himself with such issues. Rather, he embraced life fully. He mixed private and official public roles seamlessly in his activities, remaining fiercely loyal to his sovereign, somewhat remarkable in that Charles VII appears to have been fickle, superstitious, and insecure. In those few documents of Coeur's own authorship, he called himself

Jacques Coeur's motto and coat of arms. Chapel of Bourges house. (Kathryn L. Reyerson)

"counselor and *argentier* of the king" ("*conseiller et argentier du roi*"). There is no doubt about Coeur's commitment to the recovery of French lands from the English, reflecting the evolving French national sentiment of the late Middle Ages. There is no better means of characterizing Coeur than with his own motto: "For the valiant of heart, nothing is impossible" ("*A vaillans cuer riens impossible*").[8] He had this motto inscribed in several places in his magnificent house in Bourges, trumpeting the bold optimism and valor that it implies. Because of his many strengths and his few weaknesses, he was the epitome of the energy, egotism, and ambition evident in his motto.

Chapter 1 examines the fifteenth century to provide a framework for the life and experience of Jacques Coeur, while his childhood, family ties, and formative years are explored in Chapter 2. Chapter 3 features the blossoming of Coeur's career as a royal servant. His focus on Mediterranean trade and his roles as royal financier and ambassador occupy Chapters 4 and 5. The late medieval society of Coeur's time and the home and fortune he built for his family, the subject of Chapter 6, provide some measure of the man. Chapter 7 chronicles his precipitous fall from power and his escape from prison. Chapter 8 traces the end of Coeur's life in his last great adventure on crusade. A final chapter of conclusions evaluates the man and his reputation.

---

[8] Du Clercq, 617, renders the motto, "A Coeur vaillant, riens impossible."

Facade of Bourges house. (Kathryn L. Reyerson)

The Transitional Fifteenth Century

Jacques Coeur (b. 1395–1400, d.1456) was a man of the fifteenth century, a period of transition from a time historians since then have termed the Middle Ages to what is now called the early modern era, the period of the Renaissance and the Reformation. Foremost among the reasons for the transitions of the fifteenth century in Europe were warfare and shifting politics, as well as exploration. By way of introduction to the world of Jacques Coeur, these themes will be examined briefly here.

With the opening of the fifteenth century, France had been at war for almost six decades. By 1337 when England began the Hundred Years War, France had long enjoyed a stable monarchy thanks to the reign of the Capetian dynasty, founded in 987 by Hugh Capet, and crafted by 14 generations of kings, who succeeded from father to son. From the weak entity centered in Paris and the surrounding Ile–de–France region in the tenth century that was outmatched by independent neighboring principalities such as the county of Champagne-Blois, the duchy of Normandy, and the county of Anjou, the kingdom of France expanded territorially beginning with the reign of King Philip Augustus (1180–1223). Since the eleventh-century conquest of England by William the Conqueror, duke of Normandy, English kings had held French lands. In the twelfth and thirteenth centuries under the Angevin kings of England, much of western French territory, including Normandy, was in the hands of the English. It was

Philip Augustus who wrested territories in western France from King John of England (1199–1216), notably Normandy, Anjou, Poitou, and the Maine, though some lands in southwestern France, such as the Guyenne, remained in English hands. The Albigensian Crusade against Cathar heretics in the south of France brought additional lands to the French monarchy through conquest. These territories were then organized into the administrative districts or *sénéchaussées* of Beaucaire-Nîmes and Carcassonne-Béziers in 1229 and, finally, the *sénéchaussée* of Toulouse, after the death in 1271 of the king's brother, Alfonse of Poitiers, and his wife, the Toulousain heiress. Provence in southeastern France was added under Louis XI (1461–1483) in 1481. Louis XIV (the Sun King, 1643–1715) completed the current French hexagon with the addition of Alsace and Roussillon in the late seventeenth century. (See map on p. 13.)

Although Louis IX (Saint Louis, 1226–1270) gave back some western French lands to his first cousin, King Henry III of England (1216–1272), most of modern France west of the Rhône River was in the hands of the French monarchy by the year 1300. A succession crisis threatened these territorial achievements at the death, without a male heir, of Charles IV (1322–1328), the last Capetian king, in 1328. (See the accompanying genealogy.) In the end Philip of Valois (1328–1350), the scion of a collateral dynasty, the Valois, and a descendant of a brother of Philip IV (the Fair, 1285–1314), inherited the French throne. This succession had the advantage of keeping the monarchy in the male line. However, there was a closer descendant of Charles IV, in the person of his nephew Edward, son of Philip IV's daughter, Isabella of France, who married King Edward II of England (1307–1327). Edward III (1327–1377) challenged the right of the Valois dynasty to the French throne. With his pedigree, Edward III believed himself the rightful heir of the Capetians. However, French lawyers and politicians found it inconceivable that the English could inherit the French monarchy. Later in the fourteenth century French jurists established that the French throne could pass only through the male line, thus eliminating Edward III's claim through his mother. Before this, in the 1330s, Edward III pushed his rights through territorial aggression, giving rise in 1337 to the beginnings of the Hundred Years War.

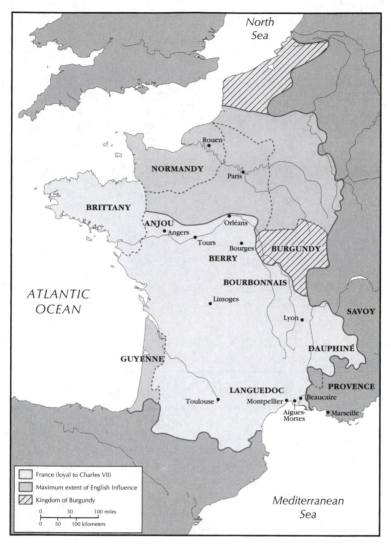

North
Sea

Rouen

NORMANDY

Paris

BRITTANY

ANJOU

Angers

Orléans

Tours

Bourges

BURGUNDY

BERRY

BOURBONNAIS

ATLANTIC
OCEAN

Limoges

Lyon

SAVOY

DAUPHINÉ

GUYENNE

PROVENCE

LANGUEDOC

Toulouse

Montpellier

Beaucaire

Aigues-
Mortes

Marseille

France (loyal to Charles VII)
Maximum extent of English Influence
Kingdom of Burgundy

0   50   100 miles
0   50   100 kilometers

Mediterranean
Sea

Medieval France in 1429.

In the irony of history, though the French won the war, they consistently lost the battles: Crécy in 1346, Poitiers in 1356, where King John of France himself was captured and had to be ransomed at great cost according to chivalric practices, and Agincourt in

KINGS OF FRANCE AND ENGLAND
(THIRTEENTH–FIFTEENTH CENTURIES)

FRANCE
PHILIP AUGUSTU (PHILIP II)
(1180–1223)
LOUIS VIII (1223–1226)
SAINT LOUIS (LOUIS IX)
(1226–1270)
PHILIP III (1270–1285)
PHILIP THE FAIR (PHILIP IV)
(1285–1314)
LOUIS X (1314–1316)
PHILIP V (1316–1322)
CHARLES IV (1322–1328)
PHILIP VI OF VALOIS (1328–1350)
JOHN THE GOOD (1350–1364)
CHARLES V (1364–1380)
CHARLES VI (1380–1422)
CHARLES VII (1422–1461)
LOUIS XI (1461–1483)

ENGLAND
JOHN (1199–1216)
HENRY III (1216–1272)
EDWARD I (1272–1307)
EDWARD II (1307–1327)
EDWARD III (1327–1377)
RICHARD II (1377–1399)
HENRY IV (1399–1413)
HENRY V (1413–1422)
HENRY VI (1422–1461)
EDWARD IV (1461–1483)

GENEALOGY

PHILIP THE FAIR (PHILIP IV) (1285–1314)			CHARLES OF VALOIS + MARGUERITE OF ANJOU
			PHILIP VI OF VALOIS (1328–1350)
			JOHN THE GOOD (1350–1364)

| LOUIS X (1314–1316) | PHILIP V (1316–1322) | CHARLES IV (1322–1328) | ISABELLA OF FRANCE + | EDWARD II (1307–1327) EDWARD III (1327–1377) |

1415, made famous later in Shakespeare's play *Henry V*. In each of these encounters the flower of French chivalry, armored knights mounted on mighty steeds, were tactically outmatched by the new technology of medieval warfare, urban militia with pike and long bow, skilled archers from a tradition of archery that developed on village greens where recreation and amusement involved contests of marksmanship. The French first experienced such a defeat at the hands of Flemish townsmen at the battle of Courtrai in 1302, but it was another 150 years before they learned the lesson that time and military technology had outstripped the glorious medieval knight, so ingrained was chivalric warfare in the consciousness of the French and Burgundians. Knighthood carried mystique and glamor. The crusades had given the knight a religious credibility as well. Noble ethos and culture were very influential in France as the nobility was the prominent social group, and tradition was strong. Change came only slowly and with difficulty.

It was not military backwardness alone that handicapped the French. The king of France Charles VI (1380–1422) suffered periodic bouts of madness that became ever more frequent after 1392. His reign was troubled, first, by the early dominance of his uncles, including John, duke of Berry, the builder of the Sainte-Chapelle and ducal palace in Bourges, and Philip the Bold, duke of Burgundy, and then under a period of governance by the king's advisors, the Marmousets, who assisted him after he, at age 20, sent his uncles away. The king's younger brother Louis, duke of Orléans, remained loyal to him. The Marmousets placed great store by royal service and reform and made themselves unpopular with the royal family, causing tension between these groups. The watershed came with the onset of Charles' mental crisis in the forest of Le Mans in 1392. The Marmousets bore the brunt of responsibility since they were closest to the king; they fled, and Charles' uncles returned to influence the course of government. From this moment, the king, beset by madness, ruled with diminishing effectiveness, leaving the door open to the later factionalism that split France in two.

In the vacuum that emerged, divisions grew between the Burgundians, under the leadership first of Philip the Bold, then from 1404 of his son, John the Fearless, in the north and east, on the one hand, and, on the other, the party that came to be known as the Arma-

gnacs in central and southern France, initially led by Louis of Orléans, who was married to Valentine Visconti, daughter of the lord
of Milan, of the great Italian house of Visconti. These two rival nobles, John the Fearless and Louis of Orléans, vied for influence over
the debilitated king, whose frustration grew ever greater as he
lapsed in and out of sanity. The sons of another of the king's uncles,
Louis of Anjou, were in control of the Maine, Anjou, and Provence
(not a French province at the time). The duke of Berry, in his last
years, governed the French provinces of the Berry, the Angoumois,
the Périgord, the Blésois, and the Dunois. In spite of political crisis
this was a brilliant period of French culture, in art, architecture, and
literature, under the patronage of great noble houses. Painters free
of foreign influence came to the fore in the persons of the Limbourg
brothers. Christine de Pisan (ca. 1364–ca. 1430), albeit of Italian
origin, emerged as the first French woman of letters.

Hostilities surfaced in earnest when hoodlums in the employ of
the Burgundian party assassinated Louis of Orléans in 1407.
Count Bernard VII of Armagnac succeeded Louis of Orléans as the
leader of the Orléanist/Armagnac faction. The Armagnacs were
committed to avenging the assassination of Louis. The Armagnac
party ruled the majority of French territory south of Paris, with the
exception of the southwestern province of the Guyenne, still in
English hands, but including the whole of the Mediterranean coast
of what was then France. Though the distraught king attempted to
make peace among members of the royal family, the lines of civil
war had been drawn. A period of anarchy, coinciding with the
childhood of Jacques Coeur, ensued. Hostilities between the Armagnacs and Burgundians broke out in 1411.

The **Cabochien revolt** followed in 1413, when a popular party
of Burgundians led by a slaughterhouse worker, Simon Le
Coustellier (nicknamed Caboche), took over parts of Paris and
held the queen and the heir to the throne, or dauphin, hostage
along with others of the royal family. Butchers were traditionally
rich and powerful in medieval cities that were always in need of
food. At this time in Paris, the butchers, along with the wine merchants, were supportive of the Burgundian party and cultivated
by Dukes Philip the Bold and John the Fearless. The result of the
revolt was Charles VI's promulgation, in a *lit de justice*, a very
important session of the high court, the *Parlement de Paris*, with

the king present, of the so-called **Cabochien ordinance** demanding wide-sweeping general reforms within the kingdom. Pressure from Armagnac lords outside Paris and from moderate elements within brought about an agreement on 28 July 1413; the ringleaders of the revolt fled Paris, and in another *lit de justice* the reforming ordinance was abolished. Such political crises only enhanced the difficulties of these decades of war for the French.

The great French defeat by the English at the Battle of Agincourt (1415) followed shortly thereafter. The Armagnac party avenged the assassination of the duke of Orléans by a second assassination, that of John the Fearless, duke of Burgundy, in 1419. John the Fearless had withheld his support and that of his son from the French king at the battle of Agincourt, and the duke's refusal to adopt an anti-English position angered the party of the **dauphin** Charles (the future Charles VII, 1422–1461), born in 1403, the eleventh of 12 children and youngest son of King Charles VI of France and Queen Isabeau of Bavaria. He succeeded an older brother as heir to the French crown in 1417. Burgundian influence grew ever stronger in northern France after the Agincourt defeat, and John the Fearless took over Paris in May–June 1418, sparking another revolt under the executioner **Capeluche**. During a meeting on 10 September 1419 between Charles and John the Fearless, a member of Charles' entourage stabbed the duke of Burgundy to death on the bridge at Montereau. This act reinforced the hostilities between the Armagnacs and Burgundians. Further complicating the situation was the fact that Catherine, sister of the dauphin Charles, married King Henry V of England, to whom Charles VI willed the kingdom of France by the **Treaty of Troyes** of 21 May 1420. Charles VI thereby disinherited the dauphin Charles, an act no doubt precipitated by Henry V's demands and by the Montereau assassination. Shortly thereafter, rumors spread of the dauphin's illegitimate birth. There was, in fact, some real question about the legitimacy of Charles' birth, that is, whether he actually was the son of King Charles VI. His mother Isabeau had a reputation for affairs, but then her husband Charles VI was insane. Rumors of illegitimacy compromised Charles' claim to the French throne. He was obliged to flee Paris and chose to take refuge in Bourges in 1418. Charles VI died in 1422 as did Henry V.

The north of France, including the capital of Paris, remained in the hands of the Burgundian faction, led by Philip the Good, duke of Burgundy, and regents of the English king Henry VI, who was still a child. Henry VI had been crowned king of France in 1422 at the death of his father Henry V, who himself had become king of France, according to the Treaty of Troyes, upon the death of Charles VI. The dauphin Charles and the Armagnac faction controlled the southern half of the kingdom. Fortunes finally changed in 1429–1430 for the faction of the dauphin with the intervention of Joan of Arc, whose mission was to bring about the coronation of the dauphin as the legitimate king Charles VII.

A watershed for the French in the Hundred Years War resulted from the actions of Joan of Arc. Joan was born about 1412 in the little town of Domrémy in Lorraine in eastern France, almost on the border of German lands. Of peasant origin, she was a young woman of religious faith, imbued with mysticism. She heard voices, particularly those of the Virgin Mary and Saint Michael, who urged her to go to the assistance of Charles so that he could be crowned king. She was fiercely loyal to the dauphin, reflecting the extraordinary growth of French national sentiment far beyond the region of Paris by the late Middle Ages, an enthusiasm that Jacques Coeur and others across France shared. While local and regional orientation remained strong, a national identity was emerging in the fifteenth century. Joan's destiny was to restore the faith of the French people in their king and inspire them to further victories. She convinced military leaders in Lorraine of her mission and ultimately made her way to the court of the dauphin himself, where she gained an audience with Charles whom she identified in a crowd. Charles, sensitive to the mysticism of his time and superstitious in his own right, was impressed by Joan's predictions of victory. Though a woman, she rode with French troops and rallied them sufficiently to drive the English from the siege of the city of Orléans, south of Paris, in 1429. This victory made a huge impression on the French and on Charles himself, who had been indecisive and uncertain of his claim to the throne before that time. Joan then led Charles to Reims for his coronation and consecration as Charles VII of France on 17 July 1429, thereby establishing his legitimacy and giving the French a rallying point for the last phase of the Hundred Years War. The tradition of coronation at Reims stretched back to the Merovingian king Clovis at the end of the fifth century CE. The archbishop of Reims, Saint Rémy, consecrated Clovis with holy oil brought down from heaven by a dove, or so the tradition goes. French kings thereafter, whenever possible, were crowned at Reims, making it particularly important that Charles VII be crowned there, given the competing claim of the English kings to the throne of France.

For Joan, her exploits ended in tragedy. After Reims, she engaged in several additional battles, not all successful, was wounded and then captured at Compiègne in May 1430 by opposing troops under the bastard of Wandonne, and passed on to John of Luxembourg, who handed her over to the English for the price of 10,000 *écus*. She was taken to Rouen in upper Normandy, where she was tried by the English as a heretic. Not all Charles VII's advisors were favorably disposed to Joan; she had lost credibility after her predictions failed and she began to experience military defeat. The French did not come to Joan's rescue. At the trial presided over by Pierre Cauchon, bishop of Beauvais, under the auspices of the duke of Bedford, regent for the English and ruler of France on behalf of the young king Henry VI, Joan initially proclaimed her innocence but, under interrogation, doubted the authenticity of her voices. She soon recanted, however, and as a relapsed heretic was handed over to the secular powers to be burned at the stake in Rouen in 1431. In the nineteenth and twentieth centuries Joan enjoyed renewed renown and in 1920 was made the patron saint of France.

Though Charles VII had more battles to fight and still in 1450 was campaigning in Normandy and in 1451 in the Guyenne, French fortunes of war improved after Joan of Arc. Paris fell to the forces of Charles VII in 1436. Further campaigns span the 1440s with a climax in the fall of Normandy in 1449–1450 and the recapture of the Guyenne in 1451–1453. The Hundred Years War was a turning point in French geographic expansion. In 1453 the French drove the English from French territory, with the exception of the port of Calais on the English Channel, which remained English into the sixteenth century. Beginning with the rule of Philip the Bold of Burgundy at the end of the fourteenth century, Burgundy became almost a rival kingdom, with dual poles in Flanders in the north and the duchy of Burgundy in east central France. But the dukes of

Burgundy backed the losing side in the Hundred Years War. Now, finally, at the end of the war, the French king not only controlled France but dominated Burgundy, as Charles VII's influence over the duke of Burgundy, Charles the Good, clearly demonstrated.

The cities and countryside of France suffered enormously during the Hundred Years War since the war was fought exclusively on French soil. After each battle was over, the armies on both sides disbanded, and unemployed soldiers foraged to find their own food and necessities. The hired soldiers or mercenaries of the great companies, as the military units were called, killed people, looted homes, destroyed agriculture, and instituted a reign of terror. The English suffered casualties and faced large tax burdens to field armies, but they never had the war in their homeland. In France, war forced cities to spend enormous sums to fortify against attack, building and rebuilding walls that were not always effective. The English takeover of the whole of northern France deprived many French people of their property, which was given to English soldiers or supporters of the Anglo-Burgundian side. Upon victory the pro-English holders lost their lands, but late into the fifteenth century, long after the war ended in 1453, lawyers were still trying to sort out ownership issues. The economic burden of war in fifteenth-century France was tremendous.

In the economic crises of the late Middle Ages, Jacques Coeur assisted Charles VII in raising taxes to fund war efforts and in rationalizing royal administration. In order to win the war Charles VII had to have an army upon which he could depend. This was a very expensive enterprise and one for which France in the early fifteenth century was poorly equipped bureaucratically and fiscally. The traditional practices of earlier French kings, who had to raise an army every time there was a crisis, were ill-fitted to late medieval warfare that relied on mercenaries and professionals, costly but effective in campaigns. The pressures of the Hundred Years War led to the creation of a permanent army that had to be financed with secure royal taxes; in the forefront of developments under Charles VII were the standing army and permanent taxation. In both the collaboration of Coeur was crucial. By the 1440s, Charles VII had established a system that would be one of the building blocks of French hegemony in Europe. France and its people suffered greatly during this period of war, but, as is often the case in crisis, important changes occurred. Historians are fond of stating that France won the Hundred Years War with England (1337–1453) thanks to Charles VII, Joan of Arc, and Jacques Coeur. France emerged intact from the ordeal and went on to become an absolute monarchy and the strongest kingdom in Europe in the early modern era.

The late Middle Ages was also a formative period for the growth of the French nation. France in the early and high Middle Ages was a collection of provinces, often quite independent of the king. Gradually, the kings established a provincial administration, and gradually they were respected by the people. The Hundred Years War was a test of people's loyalty. The English kings' claim to the French throne directly challenged the French kings' rule. Increasing numbers of people came to define themselves as pro-English or pro-French, though some simply desired peace under any ruler. By the reign of Charles VII, and after his coronation, thanks in part to Joan of Arc, identification with king and kingdom began to rank with earlier and abiding loyalties to a rural community, a region, or a city. Saint Michael, Joan's saint, was a particularly powerful rallying point for the country as a whole. Joan herself contributed greatly to unifying the French spirit. The French king became the king of all the people. Jacques Coeur demonstrated an extraordinary loyalty to his king, Charles VII, and to the kingdom during his lifetime.

The transformations of the fifteenth century constructed French national identity, and the world of royal politics widened to admit men of Coeur's background, from urban families whose fortune was grounded in artisanal industry, trade, finance, or the law, and whose training included university education or practical experience in business. Often individuals of great talent, they performed admirably in royal service, and their allegiance to the king equaled their exploits on his behalf. In addition to financial gains, their rewards often included ennoblement, as did Coeur's. This group of commoners, as the core of the Third Estate, and once ennobled, members of the *noblesse de robe*, would be influential in French politics under the Ancien Régime.

In warfare and in politics the fifteenth century was a transitional era for France. In a broader sense, culminating in the 1492 voyage of Columbus, it was an era of great significance for western European exploration. The Mediterranean Sea would be the focus of Coeur's trade, diplomacy, and final crusade, but Atlantic exploration went on apace during this era; its beginnings preceded his career by about a century. (See maps on pages 23 and 24.) The exploration and mapping of the Atlantic archipelago began with European voyages to the Canaries in the 1330s. Certainly, from the late thirteenth century there had been interest in Atlantic travel, with the ill-fated voyage of the Vivaldi brothers of Genoa out into the Atlantic (they were never to return)—probably to sail around Africa rather than to cross the ocean—and thanks to the development of an Atlantic sea route between the Mediterranean and the North Sea by the Genoese and the Majorcans from the 1280s.

Beginning in the later fourteenth century, as exploration extended to the Atlantic Mediterranean (the islands of the Canaries, the Azores, Cape Verde, and the Madeiras), the major western Mediterranean powers, Aragon, and Genoa, and as time went on Castile and Portugal, pursued their traditional mercantile goals by tapping into existing trading networks from new bases or colonizing with the establishment of sugar plantations. (See map on p. 24.) Western European powers had been accustomed in the Mediterranean to founding colonies or *fondachi*. Grants of land and extraterritorial rights permitted western merchants to establish themselves in a congenial setting from which they could trade. They were always in search of spices and gold. However, in the Atlantic islands, Mediterranean techniques could not be used. Rather, there was need for settlement as these areas were uninhabited, with the exception of the Canaries, where the population was thin. There were no regimes with which the Europeans could interact. There was no indigenous trade in which to participate. Even the plantation model that had been used in the western Mediterranean for sugar exploitation could not be replicated, given the lack of population, without the importation of slaves from west Africa.

Reconquista experience and geographic proximity provided the peoples of the Iberian peninsula with advantages in the exploration of the Atlantic Mediterranean. Because of the differences between Mediterranean and Atlantic experience, Castilians and Portuguese, imbued with the success of the *Reconquista* on the Iberian peninsula, were increasingly active. Since the eleventh century Spanish energies had focused on the defeat of Muslim rule in

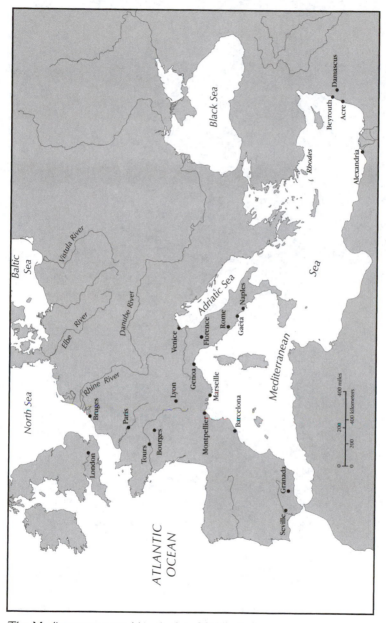

The Mediterranean world in the late Middle Ages.

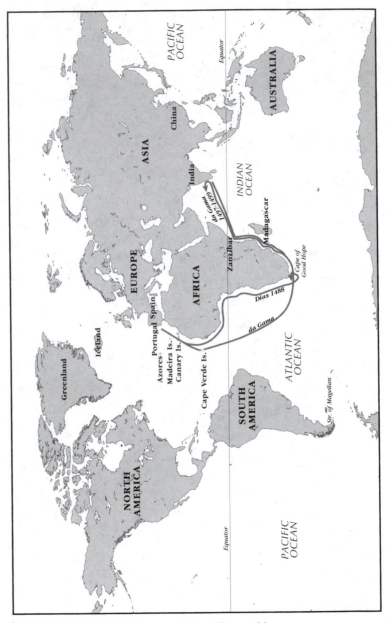

The Atlantic Mediterranean and the wider world.

Spain. As the reconquest spread south, the Spanish established settlements with Christian colonists. Italians from various cities had dominated the Mediterranean, limiting Iberian access to the markets of the Near East. In North Africa the rivalry between the Catalans and the Genoese was legendary, but in the Atlantic, Iberians had a clear geographic advantage. In the 1430s and 1440s, the heyday of Jacques Coeur's Mediterranean activities, Prince Henry the Navigator of Portugal (1394–1460)—who never navigated himself and traveled by sea in a limited fashion only—sent his sailors venturing to the Canaries in the quest for gold. The Portuguese explored the west coast of Africa for the same reasons, searching for the sources of trans-Saharan gold. Sailors laid the groundwork for later Portuguese explorers to round the Cape of Good Hope (Bartolomeu Dias in 1487–1488) and sail to India (Vasco da Gama in 1497–1499). These efforts were complicated by papal crusading bulls and the need for papal permission for conquest, the pretext being conversion, if not crusade. Portuguese efforts from 1441 turned to exploration around the bulge of Africa (the westernmost extension of the continent into the Atlantic), with considerable results by the death of Prince Henry in 1460. Though they did not penetrate the African interior, thwarted by desert and unfamiliar tropical diseases, a system of coastal trading posts, established over the next decade and a half, would yield gold, slaves, malaguetta pepper, and ivory. Jacques Coeur had no role in these ventures, but they coincided chronologically with his Mediterranean activities.

Beyond the Castilians and the Portuguese, the Crown of Aragon, the Genoese, and the French figured in the category of potential explorers in the late fourteenth and fifteenth centuries. France did not play a dominant role in early discoveries although, as a powerful monarchy, without the challenges of the Hundred Years War, it might have organized an efficient exploratory effort. Moreover, of all these countries, France was perhaps the best positioned for maritime exploration, with long seacoasts on both the Atlantic Ocean and the Mediterranean Sea. The crusading tradition in France had been fertile ground for the launching of many colonization efforts in the Near East. (See Chapter 8.) Breton and Gascon fishermen knew the north Atlantic waters. The 1390 Al-Mahdiya Crusade in Tunisia could count among its participants Jean de Béthencourt, lord of Granville on the Normandy coast, and Gadifer de la Salle of Poitiers. These two were acquainted with or related to others with Spanish and even Canaries experience, notably the duke of Orléans' chamberlain, Robert de Braquemont, who married into the Mendoza family of Castile in 1393, at a time when he could learn of the Canaries. In the early fifteenth century, with Castilian assistance, Béthencourt and de la Salle attempted the conquest of the Canaries that Béthencourt then placed under Castilian allegiance, for reasons of pragmatism and because of geographic proximity. France missed an opportunity here, but one can only wonder whether any at the court of the mad Charles VI realized this. They were preoccupied with the crisis of power in France and more generally with the Hundred Years War. There was no money for exploration, and all the funds a royal financier like Jacques Coeur could raise for the king in the 1430s and 1440s were directed to the war expenses of Charles VII.

In the era of Jacques Coeur there were also non-Europeans who might have challenged the Spanish and the Portuguese in the inauguration of an age of global exploration. Zheng He (d. 1435), the eunuch admiral of the empire of China, who was of Mongol and Muslim origin, made seven voyages in the Indian Ocean and the Persian Gulf over the period of 1405–1433. Both Zheng He's father and grandfather had experience in the Near East as they had made the holy pilgrimage to Mecca. On the first voyage of Zheng He in 1405–1407, he commanded 27,000 men and more than 300 ships, of which the largest were almost six times the size of the flag ship of Christopher Columbus in his "discovery" of the new world. Some Chinese ships were up to 440 feet long and 186 feet wide. A rudder of 11 meters has survived from one of them. The purpose of Zheng He's voyages was less that of commerce than of observation and diplomacy to spread the renown of the Chinese empire. Then, abruptly, the Ming ceased their maritime voyages, much as the Mongols had suddenly retreated from eastern Europe in 1240. The Ming feared further Mongol invasions from the north and put their energies and initiatives into fortification and defense, with undertakings such as the restoration and extension of the Great Wall.

The Chinese developments in industry and military technology from about 1000 to 1433 had a great impact, however, on increases in markets throughout a large part of the world. Significantly, they fostered greater commercialism across Eurasia, which would influence the economy worldwide through the impetus for economic behavior that was regulated by the market rather than by political power. Market-regulated behavior was most influential in Europe where the emergence of economic processes and structures encouraged European expansion. Leaving this impressive legacy, the Chinese turned inward after the 1430s.

Besides the Ming, additional peoples who might have challenged the Iberians in the early discovery era faced significant obstacles to their pursuit of maritime exploration. The Mongol empire of Asia had broken up, leaving the Mongols fragmented and in decline. The Mughals were occupied with land expansion in India. The Ottoman Turks were engaged in the creation of a vast land empire. Thus, it fell to the Europeans, and first to the Iberians, to begin the so-called discovery of the world. A search for wealth in the spices of Asia and the gold of Africa drove these explorations. But there were underlying religious motives too: crusade, proselytization, conversion to Christianity, and the search for the legendary kingdom of Prester John, that shadowy Christian king of some far-off land to the east or the south of Europe.

It is against this fifteenth-century background of war, politics, and exploration that Jacques Coeur's life and contributions in France, in Europe, and in the Mediterranean world must be set. His earliest years provide the first clues to his future actions and success.

Childhood and Family in Bourges

Jacques Coeur was born between 1395 and 1400 in the city of Bourges in the Berry, a province in north-central France, south of the Loire River and west of Burgundy, in the modern department of the Cher. (See map on p. 13.) Today the train takes one from Paris to Bourges in a little over two hours. From the perspective of fifteenth-century Bourges, Paris was the distant and very large capital of the kingdom of France. About 220 kilometers separate the capital from Bourges, a journey of a good seven days at the caravan merchant's rate of about 30–35 kilometers a day, and probably at least three days for a messenger on horseback. Although by the late Middle Ages what happened in Paris was significant for all the French, regional loyalties remained strong, as Coeur's life exemplifies. Indeed, it was friends and acquaintances from his early experience in Bourges and the Berry who provided business associates and trusted collaborators throughout his career. It was at Bourges that Coeur built his palace, which rivaled the homes of kings. (See photo on p. 10.) By the same token, the presence of the household of John, duke of Berry (1340–1416), and for a period, that of Charles VII, the "king of Bourges," created unique business opportunities for the mercantile elite of Bourges, of which Coeur was a product.

The town of Bourges, in which Coeur spent his childhood, adolescence, and young adulthood, enjoyed some renown in the Middle Ages. The Valois kings placed considerable store by

Bourges before it became a royal capital under the dauphin Charles, heir to the French throne, and the Armagnac party in 1418. Already in the later fourteenth century Duke John of Berry built one of his many palaces there. His most famous castle, Mehun-sur-Yèvre, known to modern readers from the illuminations of the Limbourg brothers' book of hours, *Les Très Riches Heures,* was located not far from Bourges.[1] By the year 1400, the skyline of Bourges was marked by significant monuments, including the cathedral of Saint-Etienne, the Sainte-Chapelle, built by the duke of Berry for his tomb and consecrated in 1405, and a large tower in the upper sector of the town not far from the ducal palace.[2]

The merchants and artisans who supplied the markets of Bourges profited greatly from the needs over decades of the household of the duke of Berry and were all the more enriched and stimulated by the installation of the court of the dauphin. Charles VII retained a presence in Bourges and in the west of France, even after Paris was reconquered from the English in 1436. The opportunities for entry into royal service multiplied for young inhabitants of Bourges.

Coeur was born into a mercantile family that fifteenth-century chroniclers described as poor and plebian to contrast it with the elevated station he ultimately achieved.[3] In fact, however, his family origin was not modest within a medieval urban context. His father Pierre was a furrier probably from Saint-Pourçain-sur-Sioule, a town in the province of the Bourbonnais,

---

[1]The *Très Riches Heures* is one of the most famous medieval devotional manuscripts, with illuminations (miniature paintings) illustrating activities of the 12 months of the year. The three Limbourg brothers, Paul, Jean, and Herman, probably working for the duke of Berry, left this work unfinished at their deaths in 1416.

[2]A fire destroyed a large number of houses and churches in 1487. Most of the Municipal Archives of Bourges also went up in flames in this fire, depriving historians of much specific information about the early years of Jacques Coeur and about the history of his family and their connections in Bourges. Other archives—those of regional administrative organs, the *bailliage,* the *prévôté,* the salt storage facilities, and the notarial archives—have also disappeared. The ducal chapel was damaged in a fire and a storm in the eighteenth century and torn down.

[3]Mollat, 350, enumerated the various fifteenth-century characterizations of Coeur's background.

southeast of the Berry. His mother is said to have been the daughter or the widow of a butcher named Jean Baquelier, before she married Pierre Coeur. The latter scenario would appear likely. It may be that she had children by her first marriage, as suggested in the attached family tree. (see p. 32.) A younger Jean Baquelier has been identified by some as a half-brother of Coeur, by others as a cousin.[4] Coeur had a younger brother, Nicolas, born about 1403, and also a sister, whose name has not survived. Nicolas had a university degree in **canon law** (*licenciatus in decretis*) as early as 1428. He entered the Church and became a canon (cathedral priest) of the cathedral of Bourges and of the Sainte-Chapelle of the duke of Berry. Nicholas served as a royal attorney at the papal court from 1438 to 1443, after which he was appointed bishop of Luçon. He was instrumental at significant moments in Coeur's career, particularly in regard to his entrees at Florence and in papal circles in Rome. Nicolas acted as a go-between for his brother in his acquaintance with Pope Eugenius IV (1431–1447). Nicolas was also a friend and correspondent of King Charles VII's confessor, Gérard Machet, facilitating another avenue of access to the royal court. These ecclesiastical connections were very important for Coeur throughout the later decades of his career. Jean Baquelier, his cousin or half-brother, was also a canon at Bourges, where he remained until his death in 1475. Association with the cathedral of Bourges was an abiding passion for Coeur; he constructed a sacristy and a funerary chapel for his family there. Coeur's sister made an important marital alliance with the notary Jean Bochetel of a family from Reims, secretary to the king and then to the dauphin Louis XI. She had a daughter, Perrette, Coeur's niece, who married a young associate and loyal collaborator of Coeur, Jean de Village. Thus, Coeur's brothers had significant careers, and his sister made an impressive marriage.

At the time of Pierre Coeur's marriage with the widow Baquelier, the family, which included the child, Jean Baquelier, may have occupied a house of hers, perhaps inherited from her first hus-

---

[4]Jean-Yves Ribault called him a half-brother; Michel Mollat preferred to designate him a cousin. Ribault's arguments seem convincing. Ribault unearthed a document that named Jean Baquelier as the uncle of Geoffroy Coeur, son of Jacques.

COEUR FAMILY TREE

Mother N + Jean Baquelier (first husband, +1395–1400) ‖
+ second husband Pierre Coeur

Jean Baquelier,	other sibling?	COEUR	Nicolas	N (sister)
(ca. 1395, +1475)		(ca. 1395–1400–1456)	(ca. 1403–1451)	+ Jean Bochetel
		+ ca. 1420 Macée de Léodepart (+1452)		

Jean	Henri	Geoffrey	Ravand	Perrette
(ca. 1421 –1483)	(ca. 1429)	(+ 1488) + 1463 Isabeau Bureau		+ 1447 Jacquelin Trousseau

band, the butcher, near the Yèvrette stream in a quarter of Bourges frequented by tanners, **drapers**, and fullers, good contacts, certainly, for the furrier Pierre. Much later, at the end of his life, Jean Baquelier bequeathed this same house to the cathedral chapter to which he had been attached for his whole career. At some point in Coeur's childhood, his father Pierre moved the family household from this outlying area of Bourges to the vicinity of the ducal palace in a prestigious quarter not far from the Sainte-Chapelle. As early as 1409, Pierre rented a house at the corner of the present-day streets the rue d'Auron and the rue des Armuriers. The Coeur family seems ultimately to have occupied two houses at this location. Coeur is said to have been associated with the ducal chapel during his childhood, perhaps spending time in a chapel choir or school run by priests. He certainly acquired the basics of reading, writing, and arithmetic, but the specifics of his schooling are unknown. There were public schools in Bourges, under ecclesiastical direction, open to urban children at this time. The nineteenth-century historian Pierre Clément published a small collection (the originals now lost) of Coeur's letters from his later life, some carrying an elaborate, if rather hesitant signature. It is likely that as an ecclesiastic, Coeur's brother Nicolas was more highly educated, but the education of Nicolas, licensed in canon law, indicates the commitment of their father Pierre to education and his ability to pay for it. It is likely that Coeur also benefited from some educational background. Coeur's extraordinary success in business and royal service, his relationship with Pope Nicholas V (see Chapter 8), a patron of humanists and scholars of his age who is credited with restructuring the Vatican Library, his friendship with Charles VII's confessor, Gérard Machet, his contacts with kings of his age point to his ability to communicate with the educated and the powerful. Albert Boardman Kerr made the argument that Coeur was literate in Latin and French on the basis of surviving correspondence.

Beyond his education, neighborhood contacts near the Sainte-Chapelle and the palace of the duke of Berry were significant for Coeur in his later career. The Varye family of drapers—cloth merchants—who lived in the same area of town as the Coeurs, furnished Coeur with a close associate and lifelong friend, Guillaume de Varye, and another associate, Simon de Varye, his younger brother. The Varyes were sons of Renaud de Varye, who had made significant loans to the king. Guillaume would be Coeur's main assistant, his principal **factor**, closely involved in his affairs, serving as principal clerk of the *Argenterie* for a time before the arrest of Coeur when Guillaume fled to Valencia in Spain and later to Italy. Guillaume was also ennobled in the late 1440s. Early in the reign of Louis XI in 1461, Guillaume succeeded to some of Coeur's positions as vicar general of finance in Languedoc, royal valet, and head of the *Argenterie*. Guillaume de Varye made a brilliant marriage with Charlotte de Bar, the daughter of Lord Jean de Bar of Baugy.

In addition to the Varye family, the Village were also close neighbors of the Coeurs. The Village were another family of drapers in Bourges whose association with Coeur and his business was a lifelong affair. The elder Jean, a master draper, died before 1444. He and his brother Guillaume de Village lived in adjacent town houses near the present Place des Quatre Piliers. A younger collaborator, Jean de Village, probably the son of the above Jean, was also a factor (assistant) of Coeur and served as one of his ship captains. From childhood, and from his quarter of Bourges near the ducal palace, Coeur made connections that would last a lifetime. He arranged the marriage of Jean to his sister's daughter, Perrette. Jean was established in Marseille from the late 1440s when Coeur moved his southern French business from Montpellier to Marseille. He remained there during the imprisonment of Coeur. These two colleagues, Guillaume de Varye and Jean de Village, are representative of the close-knit associates upon whom Coeur relied throughout his career. They were highly competent, completely trustworthy, and remarkably loyal at the time of Coeur's downfall. The acquaintances and friends of his youth and the actual location in Bourges of their houses remained dear to Coeur, who built his own palace in the same area at the end of his career. (See photo on p. 10.) Coeur had as many as ten properties in Bourges in later life.

Coeur's first attachments were forged in the region of the Berry in central France. This type of bond was typical of the Middle Ages. Most medieval inhabitants lived, worked, married, and died within a relatively small territory that the French historian Claude Gauvard has termed "the region where one was known" ("*pays de connaissance*"). For Coeur, this territory had its center in Bourges and the mercantile milieu from which his family sprang. Over time it expanded to include the Berry and may have extended as far as the Bourbonnais, from which his father came. Coeur's rather heavy real estate investment in the Bourbonnais suggests that he was drawn to this region as well as to the Berry. (See Chapter 6.)

The relationships Coeur entertained with family, friends, and acquaintances laid the groundwork for his activities. The foundation of Coeur's support was familial. Members of the Coeur family helped each other out, suggested clearly in the way the **canonates** of the cathedral of Bourges and the Sainte-Chapelle, lucrative ecclesiastical offices, passed among his sons and brothers. The Middle Ages placed enormous emphasis on blood ties. Business relations were often underpinned by close family ties. Coeur arranged marriages between his own family members and his associates, Jean de Village, and another of his ship captains, Guillaume Gimart, who married a Coeur cousin, Jeanne Heymar. Beyond blood ties, clienteles, groups of individuals who operated together in concert in social, political, and business contexts, were very significant in the medieval and early modern periods. A merchant entourage could include non-family members as well as family. Here the relationships were also close. It is often difficult to separate ties of friendship from ties of clientage in these eras.

Generally, friendship suggested a footing of equality while client-age often implied a vertical hierarchy, with reciprocal obligations. Coeur used family and childhood contacts as his closest confidants; then, in radiating circles of attachment, he reached out to more distantly connected people in his employ. The foundation of his friendships varied according to circumstances and individuals. Coeur's network of connections was dense, and his ties of family and friendship from Bourges were the nucleus of his organization. Coeur's arrest, trial, and condemnation, as well as his escape from prison, present a unique opportunity to observe the nature of his interactions with his entourage and others highly placed within European society at a moment of crisis. (See Chapter 7.)

These friends, Coeur, his brother Nicolas, half-brother Jean Baquelier, and Guillaume de Varye, at the least—Jean de Village was somewhat younger—had the winding streets of Bourges, lined with half-timbered houses, to explore. The medieval town grew up on an ancient site, inhabited for more than 2000 years. The street layout of Bourges, established early in the Middle Ages, remained visible in the topography of the later medieval town as it expanded during its heyday. At the time of King Philip Augustus (1180–1223), a large rampart was constructed, dramatically increasing the walled space of the fourth-century Gallo-Roman fortifications. In spite of the 1487 fire, the old town of Bourges is well preserved today, providing the modern observer with views that were probably those of Coeur and his boyhood pals. They may have marveled at the great thirteenth-century Gothic cathedral of Saint-Etienne, which still dominates the cityscape, rising as it does, in characteristic medieval fashion, out of a tight cluster of houses. The tympanum of its central portal depicts the Last Judgment: Sinners are skewered by demons; the saved, in contrast, have attained a heavenly peace, an object lesson to medieval believers, including adolescent boys. Coeur and his friends would certainly have admired the opulence of the ducal palace and the Sainte-Chapelle. Smaller church towers also dotted the cityscape known to Coeur and his friends.

Evidence suggests that medieval children and teenagers enjoyed a number of games and sports that persist today: blind man's bluff, wrestling, acrobatics, a variety of bat and ball games, dice, and throwing games such as quoits and kayles. They played at follow the leader and hide and seek. Riding hobby-horses, playing on swings and see-saws, and spinning tops were also pastimes for medieval youth. Less familiar but extremely popular in the Middle Ages were bear-baiting, the staging of impromptu cock fights, and performing horses and bears, sights to be found in the public squares of many a medieval city. The Bourges of Coeur's early years was no exception.

The countryside was not far from the center of Bourges. One passed beyond the fortifications through modest suburbs to the rolling fields of the Berry. Here, too, Coeur probably roamed with childhood friends. Swimming, catching butterflies and small song-birds, pilfering fruit from orchards, and ice skating and sledding in the winter were common outdoor activities for youths like Coeur and his friends. That Coeur remained forever attached to Bourges and the Berry is evident from his retention of numerous properties in Bourges, and his later real estate investments and building program, notably his own palace in Bourges in later life. He also acquired many châteaux in this region. Today 18 châteaux, many of them formerly in Coeur's hands, if only briefly, make up what is called the tourists' "Route Jacques Coeur."

In the mercantile quarter of a medieval city like Bourges, family living quarters were located on the second floor of the house, above the shop, warehouse, or workshop of the family business. Growing up the son of a furrier, in a neighborhood where drapers were also common, Coeur acquired an expertise in merchandising and a likely hands-on experience of the artisan activities supporting the fur and drapery businesses in the ateliers of his father and his neighbors. The trade in furs of a great variety of animals was very active in the Middle Ages. The nobility and the urban elite sought to buy them for their warmth and elegance. Furriers were makers and marketers of furs and fur-trimmed garments, robes, and bed covers. They knew their products and the producers, the skinners of furs and tanners of hides. Drapers were involved in the making and marketing of clothes. They might trim their products with furs. They were thoroughly acquainted with the different qualities of cloth and with its production process. The textile industry, particularly that of wool cloth, was the medieval urban industry par excellence. The Berry region supported sheep raising, and a sheep was featured on the town coat of arms of Bourges. The cloth of the

Berry had a reputation for quality at French fairs and was exported as far afield as Florence by the fourteenth century. It was typical of sons to follow fathers in their family business through formal apprenticeship with a father's colleague or through informal training at home. In the case of furs and cloth, Coeur gained an apprenticeship, whether formal or informal, in the production process and in regional and long-distance trade as well as local marketing.

There was money to be made in fur garments and in decorative furs applied to clothing. A furrier like Coeur's father Pierre must have done well to have been able to secure an education and a career in the Church for Coeur's brother Nicolas and good marriages for his daughter and Coeur. (See below.) Church placement was costly and **dowries** and **dowers** were expensive. In the Middle Ages, the merchant-bankers of Italian towns or the cloth entrepreneurs of Flanders and northern France were among the wealthiest of nonnoble urban inhabitants, but Pierre Coeur must have had an impressive fortune for a furrier. The butchers' connection on Coeur's mother's side also reflected a solid and often lucrative urban occupation. As a canon and later bishop, Nicolas was a member of the higher clergy, the elite of the church. The dowry for Coeur's sister's wedding to a royal notary and secretary to the future King Louis XI would have been large. Coeur himself married into a family associated with ducal and royal administration.

In fact, the Berry and his home town of Bourges provided Coeur with more than lifelong friends and invaluable mercantile, artisan, and business training. About 1418–1420, between the ages of 18 and 23, Coeur married a woman from his own quarter of Bourges, Macée de Léodepart, daughter of Lambert de Léodepart, whom he had probably known throughout his youth. Lambert's house was across the street from the Coeur house at the corner of the rue des Armuriers and the rue d'Auron. Lambert was a valet in the entourage of John, duke of Berry, a position of some social importance; Lambert would later become royal provost of Bourges. Macée's mother, Jeanne Ronsard, was also well connected. Her father, Macée's maternal grandfather, had been master of the mint in Bourges, which coined royal money. Macée's family associated as employees with members of the extended French royal family. Macée brought Coeur a dowry of various properties and real estate rents that undoubtedly aided him in his early career.

Coeur's marriage with Macée was a good match for a furrier's son, a reflection of his prospects and a testimony to the considerable commercial success of his father. In Coeur's case Lambert de Léodepart, representative of royal/ducal officialdom, was willing to unite his daughter with the family of a wealthy neighbor, Pierre Coeur, though the latter occupied a less elevated social position as a furrier. The presence of the ducal court and the royal court heightened the possibility of such a match. Then, too, fathers could arrange marriages, and young people might encounter one another. Given the attention paid to Macée's identity in the palace that Coeur would construct in Bourges at the end of his career, there is reason to believe the marriage of Coeur and Macée was one of affection as well as connections.

Coeur's marriage was early for a man of middling mercantile or artisanal background. In spite of the cliché of early marriage in the Middle Ages, in northern French towns there was a preference for marriage in the later twenties, as there was a need on the part of both spouses to acquire some standing in their occupations before marriage and children. But marriage patterns differed according to social station. Macée's age of marriage is not known, though for a woman of her heritage in the ducal and royal entourage, as opposed to artisanal or middle-class background, marriage in her teens may not have been unusual. Coeur's marriage above his family station and into a privileged family attached to royal administrative circles would be important for his future success. He was able to build his early career on the mercantile heritage of his own family and on the financial and administrative background of the family of his wife.

The marriage of Macée de Léodepart and Coeur was long and fruitful. They had five children who survived to adulthood. (See the Coeur family tree.) The family of Coeur and Macée, ennobled in 1441, was upwardly mobile. Son Jean, born about 1421, held numerous canonates at the cathedral of Bourges, at the Sainte-Chapelle, and at Saint-Martin of Tours, acquired the title of apostolic notary in 1444, and became archbishop of Bourges in 1450; he died in 1483. Jean attended university in Paris (the Faculté des Arts), receiving a law degree reflecting his competence in both canon (Church) and civil law (*in utroque jure*). Henri, born about 1429, finished his career as dean and canon of the cathedral of Limoges. In 1440 Henri resigned his canonate at the Bourges cathedral, and the prebend attached to it, in favor of his uncle Jean Baquelier. The canonate at the Sainte-Chapelle of Bourges that Coeur's brother Nicolas and then his sons Jean and Henri had held also passed to Jean Baquelier about the year 1460. Church connections, fostered through his brothers and sons, would be of great significance throughout Coeur's career. Most powerful noble families placed sons in the Church, and the urban commercial elite from which the Coeurs sprang followed suit. Following a secular trajectory, son Geoffrey, whose date of birth is unknown, became the lord of La Chaussée, among other territories, and in 1463 married Isabeau Bureau, daughter of the lord of Monglas, of a powerful family. His acquisition of a landed title and his brilliant marriage suggest the persistent power of the Coeur family after the condemnation of Coeur in 1453. Geoffrey died in 1488. Of Coeur's sons, only Ravand Coeur, the fourth son, whose dates of birth and death are unknown, went into business and worked with Coeur directly, but without the skill of his father. He did not inherit his father's genius. As his father's collaborator, he suffered directly the effects of Coeur's fall from power. Ravand cut a pathetic figure after the imprisonment and condemnation of his father and at one point threw himself on the mercy of the lawyer Jean Dauvet, appealing for means of subsistence following the confiscation of his father's goods. Dauvet gave him some funds with which he had stylish clothes fashioned. Finally, Macée and Coeur had a daughter, Perrette (sharing this name with Coeur's niece), who married Jacquelin Trousseau, son of a minor noble, the viscount of Bourges, in 1447. When widowed sometime before 1471, Perrette joined the Poor Clares, a **Franciscan** religious order in Bourges. Macée died in 1452, four years before Coeur's death in 1456.

The lives of Coeur, Macée, and their children, and those of all French people, were colored by the war and unrest of the later Middle Ages. The Hundred Years War, pitting the English against the French, opened in 1337 and involved sporadic fighting with several famous pitched battles over the course of more than a century, coming to an end finally in 1453 with the French victorious. (See Chapter 1.) By the fifteenth century France had been at war with England for more than 60 years. This was the stage upon which Coeur's career developed. He played an important role in France in the first half of the fifteenth century, doing much to facilitate Charles VII's victory over the English, but he would not reap the benefits of victory because of his 1451 arrest and 1453 condemnation.

During Coeur's childhood, the southern half of the kingdom was in the hands of the Armagnac faction, under the leadership of Count Bernard VII and the young dauphin Charles. Armagnac France far outstripped in surface area the Burgundian-held north of France; however, Burgundian France included the royal capital of Paris. The Berry and Bourges, Coeur's birthplace, were in Armagnac territory in central France. Coeur's adolescence and young adulthood took place against the background of unrest described in Chapter 1. Though the Coeur family lived in Bourges, not Paris, the events of the capital reverberated throughout the kingdom. The 1413 Cabochien revolt in Paris, inspired by the butcher Caboche when Coeur was a teenager, must have caused talk within the butchers' circle in Bourges to which Coeur was related through his mother. The takeover of Paris by the duke of Burgundy, John the Fearless, inspired another insurrection in 1418 led by the executioner Capeluche. Charles took refuge in the Berry when he was forced to flee Paris in 1418 and would be called in derogatory terms the "king of Bourges" after his father died in 1422 because he established his capital there. For the king this title was an insult, but for the town of Bourges the arrival of the royal court meant an explosion of market possibilities. The business of Pierre Coeur and his son Jacques benefited from the king's presence in Bourges, and, on a more personal level for Jacques, association with the ducal and royal courts enabled him to marry his wife.

The mercantile milieu of Bourges profited first from the presence of a ducal capital in the late fourteenth century and then from a royal one in the early fifteenth. Ducal and royal courts meant large entourages of followers who were potential commercial clients, resulting in much market activity at Bourges. Coeur's extended family and neighbors, butchers, furriers, and drapers through the Village and Varye families, were well placed to take advantage of the new economic opportunities created by the arrival of Charles' court. Despite the hostilities of war, in Coeur's part of France communications remained open with the south, with Italy, and, more broadly, with the Mediterranean world, a source of luxury products such as silks and spices, much in demand in royal and noble circles.

The Coeurs and their associates catered to the needs of noble and royal clients. The name Coeur survives in royal accounts of this time. There is the record of a Jean Coeur selling spurs to the king in 1421 or 1422, leading to the conjecture that, given the similarity of the first names, this was actually Jacques Coeur. He was in his twenties at this time and certainly capable of trade. Regardless of the accuracy of this identification, the opportunity for close association with the king and the court must have been of immeasurable assistance in facilitating Coeur's early career. The local business environment of Bourges was one where a bright and ambitious young man could acquire invaluable expertise and make his mark.

Charles VII's negative situation as the uncrowned "king of Bourges" changed with the appearance of Joan of Arc. Those acquainted with Charles VII in Bourges, including Coeur, continued to profit greatly from royal patronage after Charles became the legitimate king, thanks to the successful effort of Joan to get him crowned at Reims.[5] Because of Joan's actions, the years 1429–1430 are considered a turning point for the Hundred Years War. Though it would take another 23 years for the French to achieve victory over the English, the tide had turned in the war with Joan's intervention, at about the same time that a mature Coeur appeared on the historical scene.

---

[5] There are no surviving links between Jacques Coeur and Joan of Arc.

III

Career Beginnings (1420s–1440s)

In the 1430s and early 1440s Jacques Coeur established the profile of merchant and royal official that would create his reputation. The diversity of his career interests was evident early on, though his areas of strength would expand and develop. The passing reference to a seller of spurs, perhaps Coeur in the early 1420s, points to a commercial vocation that grew over time. Experience within the commercial milieu of Bourges, catering to the needs and desires of the royal entourage, represented one of his advantages. Another lay in connections through his wife Macée to royal officialdom and to the royal mint at Bourges. Expertise in coinage, added to his artisanal and mercantile background, positioned Jacques for greatness. Though his Bourges upbringing offered Coeur opportunities, he also encountered and overcame adversity. The first ten years of his career were somewhat checkered. He ran afoul of the law in his minting activities and was pardoned; he experienced one of the great adventures of his life with a voyage to the eastern Mediterranean in 1432, pointing him toward trade, but he was shipwrecked and robbed on the return trip. Most of the elements of Coeur's career—official roles and merchant activities—were in place by the early 1440s.

In the late 1420s Coeur worked at the Bourges mint, owing his position, most likely, to the fact that Macée's grandfather had served as royal mintmaster at Bourges. Jacques' in-laws provided him with an entree into the spheres of local and royal administration and finance. Coeur had a practical knowledge of commercial finance from his father's occupation of furrier and from his early exposure to the provisioning of the royal court at Bourges that would have qualified him for this mint position. Jacques and his associates, colleagues more experienced in finance, Ravand le Danois, Pierre Godard, and Jean Jubin, took the mint on "farm" as mintmasters in the service of the king. It was common in the late Middle Ages and in the early modern era for individuals to bid for the right to "farm," that is, to operate in a particular administrative capacity or to collect a particular tax. The highest bidder for this privilege paid the sum due for the function or tax to the king's treasury, speculating that he could bring in more revenue or profits than he had paid for the office. The mintmasters, for example, through the control of the money supply, could increase mint output and thereby augment their personal profit, which was based on coin production. In the case of the farm of a tax, the farmer collected as much in taxes as possible, having already paid the king his due. The farmer could pressure tax payers with threats to increase their tax liability. A mint, a mine, a particular local or regional tax could be the basis for the farm. The difference between the sum bid and the actual receipts collected represented profit to the farmer. In the case of a mint, the minters retained a portion of each minting of coins as their recompense. The possibilities for abuse in the farming system were legend and generated many complaints during the *Ancien Régime* of the seventeenth and eighteenth centuries.

As mintmasters, Coeur and his associates were part independent operators, part royal officials, a mixture of activities that was a common refrain of Coeur's career. They were in charge of minting coins of good quality and were mandated by law to maintain a certain level of precious metal content in the coins. While mintmasters, Jacques and his colleagues fell victim to the temptation of manipulation of the precious metal content of the coins; in 1429 royal commissioners, responsible for the early stages of Charles VII's coinage reform, caught them in an affair of fraud. The charge against Jacques and his associates was the minting of coins of inadequate precious metal content two years earlier in 1427. This is the first unequivocal historical reference to Jacques Coeur, when he was about 30 years old. In this case 76 *écus* had been struck from a **mark** of gold at 14 and 15 carats instead of the required 70 at 18 carats. The surplus of 6 *écus* per mark became fraudulent profit for the minters, and the coins themselves were lower in precious metal than they should have been. In 1430 there was another incident of fraud in the coinage of another type of French coin, gold **royals**, at 23 carats instead of 23 3/4. These were common methods used by minters to siphon off metal for their own enrichment. As it happened, the king's mercy was great. A royal letter of pardon (***lettre de rémission***) of 6 December 1429 remitted the first monetary fraud for Coeur and his associates. Letters of pardon were a common technique of royal governance by the late Middle Ages in France. The king often derived recompense for his mercy, and he assured himself of the good feelings of his subjects, who could go on to pursue their lives. Neither the 1427 nor the 1430 incident seems to have impeded Coeur's future association with mints and monetary policy until the transgression of 1427, though forgiven by the king, was recalled at the time of Coeur's arrest in 1451. Although Coeur ran afoul of the authorities for a crime relatively common among minters, he gained invaluable formative experience that served him well later in his own and in royal financial dealings. Coeur would be influential in royal monetary reform as described below.

In fact, coinage expertise was much in demand in the Middle Ages. During the last years of the reign of Charles VI and the early years of the reign of Charles VII, France was in the grips of monetary anarchy, concentrated particularly in the years 1417–1422. France had just suffered its third major defeat in the Hundred Years War at Agincourt in 1415. Following on the defeat came the period of factionalism and civil war that set the Armagnacs against the Burgundians. When the dauphin Charles left Paris and established himself in Bourges in 1418, he coined money there in his own right. King Henry V of England, rival for the French throne, coined money at Caen in Normandy in 1417. Isabeau of Bavaria, queen of France, and partisan of the Burgundians, gave the duke of Burgundy three royal mints—those of Mâcon, Troyes, and Châlons—that were added to his own mint at Dijon in the kingdom of Burgundy. The royal mint in Paris still coined money. There were thus four major monetary authorities issuing coinage during the crisis. The precious metal content of coins declined during this era but returned to a level associated with good money in 1422. However, there were 19 mutations of the coinage of Charles VII in the years 1422–1436. Insufficient metal supplies contributed to coinage difficulties. Royal authorities ordered mutations to cope with coinage instability and a crisis of confidence in the coinage, instigated by the war. Coining money was also a way to raise revenues, as the king profited from his share in each minting. However, there is no question but that business benefited from a stable coinage. Finally, the treaty of Arras of 21 September 1435 reconciled the king of France and the duke of Burgundy, and the English were from then on in retreat in the north of France. January 1436 inaugurated a long period of monetary stability lasting until 1514. In the 1420s, Jacques Coeur experienced the monetary difficulties of the period from a professional as well as a mercantile point of view. His time at the Bourges mint made an impression on him as he called his fourth son by the unusual name of Ravand, presumably after his mint associate there, Ravand le Danois.

Following the incident of monetary fraud, Coeur continued at the Bourges mint as a mintmaster and in 1430 entered into a partnership for commercial purposes, lasting until 1439, with one of his Bourges mint associates, Pierre Godard, and Godard's brother. After the initation of this partnership and perhaps because of it, Coeur's career took another turn. He began to operate geographically in new and more ambitious ways. It is perhaps not surprising that when he decided to venture beyond Bourges; he went south to the Mediterranean coast of France that lay within the territory of Charles VII and the Armagnac faction. In 1432 in his early 30s, at an age well beyond youth, Coeur embarked upon a remarkable experience with all the makings of an adventure. He departed on a trip to the eastern Mediterranean, the Levant. Any number of motives are possible. Mediterranean trade was a lucrative affair for a young businessman with backers. Then, too, his journey may have had official overtones of a diplomatic nature.

Relations between the eastern and western Mediterranean basins had a long history in the Middle Ages by the time of Jacques Coeur. Before the European "Age of Discoveries," the Mediterranean world. (See map on p. 23.) represented the largest European arena for cross-cultural exchange. Contacts among Islamic, Jewish, and Byzantine civilizations had provided western Europeans with innovations in business techniques and access to the heritage of Greco-Roman antiquity. Merchants, pilgrims, and crusaders from Europe had visited the Near East (the Levant), which acted as an intermediary between Europe and South Asia and the Orient, the traditional eastern sources of spices, drugs, exotic fruits, nuts, silks, and other fabrics fueling the medieval international luxury trade. The pattern of this trade in its most recent incarnation was by the time of Coeur more than 500 years old and had existed in earlier forms long before the Common Era. Throughout the whole of the Middle Ages, the West had been dependent on the East for expensive luxury goods; in exchange, Europeans could offer raw materials such as lumber, iron, furs, wool cloth—first of the Low Countries but later joined by products of regional cloth industries in areas such as Languedoc—and other trade items such as weapons and slaves. To finance western purchases, gold and, in the later Middle Ages, silver often supplemented these exports. Pilgrims, Jews, Arab merchants, and European merchants of the Mediterranean coastal areas were active in this east-west exchange.

Italian cities were in the vanguard in the revival of western Mediterranean trade in the tenth and eleventh centuries. Early trade contacts of the Italo-Byzantine towns of Amalfi, Bari, Gaëta, Naples in the south of Italy, and Venice in the north linked the Italian peninsula to North Africa, Egypt, the Syrian coast, and Byzantium in the Near East. The late eleventh century inaugurated with the first crusade (1095–1099), a series of European military adventures, a fusion of pilgrimage and holy war, to reconquer the Holy Land from the Muslims, leading to the establishment of crusader principalities in the Levant (1099–1291). The commercial beneficiaries of the crusades were Genoa and Pisa, which joined Venice as the dominant Mediterranean sea powers, while the southern Italian cities were conquered by the Normans and incorporated into a monarchy that would have many rulers over time: Normans, Hohenstaufens, Angevins, and Aragonese.

The major Italian players in Coeur's era were Genoa and Venice, though Venice the Serenissima (Most Serene Republic) enjoyed the upper hand in the Levant trade, through the defeat of Genoa, the Ligurian Republic, in the War of Chioggia in the late 1370s. The coasts of Syria and Egypt remained sites of western destination in spite of crusader losses in the intervening centuries, but fallback positions for westerners developed on the eastern Mediterranean islands of Cyprus and Rhodes. Surrounded by hostile mainland territories and thus dependent on supplies brought by western merchants, the port of Famagousta in Cyprus replaced the port of Acre as a major market when this last Christian stronghold on the Syrian coast fell to the Turks in 1291. Lesser Armenia and the Byzantine Empire continued as markets in Christian hands. By 1310, Rhodes was in the hands of the knights of the Order of Saint John of Jerusalem, also known as the Hospitallers, and later as the Knights of Malta.

Over time, conditions of supply to those intermediate market sites of the Near East through the long-distance central Asian overland route—the ancient silk road—or a combination of land and sea routes around South Asia also changed, and access to silks and spices became more difficult. The civil strife within the later Byzantine Empire contributed to westerners' challenges. The disintegration of the Mongol peace further exacerbated the situation. East-west trade had benefited from the Mongol conquest of Asia under Genghis Khan (1167–1227) and the creation of a remarkably stable empire that stretched some 4000 miles from the Crimea and the Black Sea to the Pacific Ocean under the so-called Mongol peace or *pax mongolica*. From the mid-thirteenth century, envoys of popes and kings had begun to travel overland to Central Asia and China. John of Piano Carpini went to the Mongol capital of Karakorum at the behest of Pope Innocent IV (1243–1254). John of Monte Corvino, another papal emissary, left Rome in 1289 and journeyed to China via India. Niccolò and Maffeo Polo traveled to China in the 1260s, with Marco joining them for their second trip a decade later. Marco stayed and worked at the court of Kublai Khan for 18 years, returning to Venice in 1292. Other

Italian merchants ventured to China, and some were buried there. Francesco di Balduccio Pegolotti wrote a celebrated commercial manual, *The Practice of Commerce* (ca. 1310–1340), describing conditions and products for merchants, including travel to China, which he viewed as quite safe.[1] However, the Mongol peace began to disintegrate in the mid-1330s. The result of this political turmoil was a disruption of the routes of supply for spices arriving across Central Asia from South Asia and the Far East. These difficulties increased in the next century as the Ottoman Turks expanded their territorial dominance in the Near East. For Coeur the challenge would be to craft cross-cultural relations in the eastern Mediterranean to permit access to surviving Levantine spice markets.

Once in the Mediterranean world, trade was a risky business. Weather for the inland sea, however attractive, could turn vicious, causing most merchants to avoid sailing in winter months. Many Mediterranean merchants favored a coastal commerce that eliminated the need for long voyages out of sight of land. However, whether in cautious coastal trade or in long-distance direct voyages, pirates and privateers frequently threatened merchant vessels. Swashbuckling admirals shifted allegiances easily and regularly passed themselves off as merchants. By the same token, merchants themselves turned pirate on occasion in the Middle Ages. Shipwreck laws of a particular locale dictated the kind of assistance merchants could expect for vessels lost at sea, and the **law of marque** authorized retaliation for unreimbursed merchant losses from piracy, usually against fellow citizens of the perpetrators. (See Chapter 5.) Through his 1432 voyage to the Levant, Coeur became involved in many dimensions of this complex and cosmopolitan Mediterranean world.

He journeyed south to Montpellier, a large town in lower Languedoc with a long history of activities in Mediterranean trade. He took passage on the *Sainte–Marie–et–Saint–Paul*, a **galley** owned by Jean Vitalis of the southern French town of Narbonne, along with merchants of Montpellier and Narbonne, sailing to Alexandria and Beirut. While in Alexandria, Coeur decided to break off

---

[1] Francesco di Balduccio Pegolotti, *La pratica della mercatura*, ed. Allan Evans (Cambridge, Mass.: Harvard University Press, 1936).

from his shipmates and travel to Damascus in Syria, where a squire of the duke of Burgundy, Bertrandon de la Broquière, who was on a pilgrimage and scouting trip to the Holy Land, noted his presence. In writing about his trip later on, de la Broquière remarked that he had encountered a Frenchman, Jacques Coeur, at Damascus, "who since then has played an important role in France as *argentier* of the king."[2] De la Broquière reported that Coeur told him the galley of Narbonne, in which he was traveling, was due to return to Beirut where fellow passengers, the southern French merchants, where fellow passengers, the southern French merchants, were making purchases, especially spices, to load in the ship. This Burgundian squire may well have been struck by the presence of a central French merchant in the Levant. The French of the north and center of the kingdom had crusaded to the Near East, sometimes remaining in the crusader principalities, but the trade of the Levant was in the hands of Italians and southern French, who secured extraterritorial colonies (*fondachi*) in the crusaders' lands. The crusade ideal, not trade, remained vibrant for the northern French late into the Middle Ages. Coeur's death on the papal crusade to Rhodes in 1456 fits into this pattern.

For the time he was in the Levant in 1432, however, Coeur did not behave like a landlocked central Frenchman. He parted company with his southern French colleagues to journey alone to Damascus, inland some distance from the coast. This was a Muslim city, as were Alexandria and Beirut. (See map on p. 23.) Travel was dangerous everywhere in the Middle Ages, but travel in the Levant for an unaccompanied European—there are no known traveling companions for this phase of Jacques' travel—presented a particular challenge without knowledge of the local languages, as was probably his situation. Coeur showed an early interest in negotiating with Islamic culture that he later pursued on behalf of Charles VII and French trade in the eastern Mediterranean. The insights and probable contacts, gained through his extensive travel in the Near East, were informative for Coeur's future Mediterranean commercial enterprise.

As it turned out, the 1432 return voyage ended in disaster. The galley of Narbonne in which Coeur and his shipmates were traveling, loaded with valuable merchandise acquired in parts beyond the

---

[2] Mollat, 21; Heers, 32.

seas (*ultramarinis*), encountered a storm that opened a breach in the ship near Corsica, a possession of the king of Aragon. Shipwreck ensued. In a small boat (*parva barcha*) some of the survivors reached Corsica to seek help while others remained with the galley to salvage and bring to shore what they could. A captain of the island and his accomplices descended upon the shipwrecked stragglers in the manner of pirates (*more piratico*) and took everything, including their shoes and shirts. The pirates detained Jean Vitalis, owner of the vessel, and the captain, Augustin Siquardi, with a ransom of 800 gold **ducats** for Vitalis' freedom, and 100 for Siquardi's, releasing Coeur and the others with only shirts to their names. Complaints were later brought before the *Parlement* (High Court) of the king of France and the court of the queen of Aragon, but it was only much later, in the 1440s, that victims took legal action for recompense under the law of marque. (See Chapter 5.) More immediate reward was the probable bonding among captives. During the Levant trip itself or perhaps on the occasion of the shipwreck off Corsica and the victims' subsequent detainment, Coeur established friendships with some of his fellow travelers and made connections that he could invoke in future Mediterranean enterprises.

Coeur's relationship with the south of France was to be of long duration. The basis for his 1432 trip deserves investigation. Though there are only limited sources for interpretation of Coeur's motives, some light can be shed on his decision to visit the south of France. The commercially oriented, Mediterranean town of Montpellier was experiencing demographic problems at this time. The town had suffered in the later fourteenth century, with visitations of the plague, the war at its doorsteps, social unrest in Languedoc, and a local rebellion against the duke of Anjou, who was serving as royal lieutenant of the province at the end of the 1370s. After decades of difficulty, in 1432, the town **consuls** of Montpellier sent out advertising circulars across France in the dialects of targeted regions—the south of France spoke *langue d'oc* and the north *langue d'oil*—offering six years' exemption from taxes on mobile wealth to attract immigration to Montpellier. Coeur may have seen one of these advertisements and made his decision to go south to Montpellier as a land of opportunity. Certainly, the Montpellier registers of inhabitation (*registres de habitanage*) noted 298 new families from Catalonia, various parts of France, and Italy, arriving as immigrants in the years 1424–1441. Coeur may thus have been attracted to Montpellier as a possible site of business and then decided to take ship for the Levant. However, there are other possible explanations as well.

Diplomacy or pilgrimage offer alternative motives for the trip. The one witness to Coeur's presence in Damascus, Bertrandon de la Broquière, who wrote years after the trip itself, did not call him a merchant, emphasizing rather his later reputation as *argentier* of the French king. The French historian Jacques Heers has pointed out that Coeur told Bertrandon he was returning to Beirut to meet, not the merchants of southern France who were traveling on the galley of Narbonne, but four Burgundian nobles, also aboard, whose names have survived: André de Toulongeon, a knight of the **Golden Fleece**, the knightly order founded in 1429 by Duke Philip the Good of Burgundy; Pierre de Vaudrey, ducal officer; Godefroy de Troisy; and Jean de La Roë, both in the duke of Burgundy's employ.[3] These four were not among those taking part in the later law of marque indemnification proceedings of the 1440s. (Chapter 5.) The mention of these Burgundian nobles permits Heers to question whether Coeur was in the Near East in 1432 on personal commercial business at all. Heers has speculated that his trip may have involved diplomatic prospecting on behalf of a western political figure, the king of France, the duke of Burgundy, or the pope.

After his return from the Levant, Coeur was again in 1435 recorded at the Bourges mint in an accounting function for the mintmaster. It seems reasonable to admit the possibility that Coeur's travel was for royal commercial purposes and that he may have been in the king's employ all along. Then, too, his trip may have been on behalf of Charles VII for diplomatic reasons such as the planning of a crusade or a pilgrimage. Finally, one could argue that Coeur was involved in some sort of personal pilgrimage of penance in regard to his misdeed of monetary fraud at the Bourges mint. There is no evidence of his remorse, however, though Coeur was later documented on at least one pilgrimage to the monastery of Montserrat in Catalonia in 1445. Penance and remorse often

---

[3] Heers, 32.

motivated pilgrimage in the Middle Ages. In spite of alternative explanations, it seems likely that the Levant trip served as a prospecting mission for Coeur's commercial purposes in light of the partnership Coeur had formed with the Godard brothers in 1430. However, there may, in fact, have been multiple motives for Coeur's travel, the unusual nature of which needs emphasis. Regardless of the exact explanation, Coeur's experience in the Near East served to familiarize him with the arena of his later commercial enterprise.

Though the galley of Narbonne in which he had been traveling was lost, Coeur undoubtedly gained valuable exposure to the challenges of Mediterranean trade and travel during that trip. Until Jacques Coeur, the French monarchy and the French of the center and north of France had not been much invested in Mediterranean trade. In the coming years Coeur involved the king of France and men of the center and north in unprecedented commercial activities in the Mediterranean world, changing the shape of French commerce permanently. Coeur's trade created a direct link for the French monarchy, without expensive intermediaries, to the commercial riches of the Levant, hitherto in the control of Italians of the great city states of Genoa, Venice, and to a lesser degree Pisa, and of southern French and Catalans. In the immediate aftermath of his trip, however, his career took a further financial direction.

In 1436 or 1437, Coeur assumed the farm of the mint of Paris, where he became mintmaster, a position of royal appointment. Coeur's experience in monetary matters in his stints at the Bourges and Paris mints soon led him to a new official role. In 1438 he advised the king on monetary matters contributing to reform efforts to provide a more stable royal coinage and to regulate money exchange among the dozens of coinages in circulation in western Europe. The king, with Coeur's assistance, also sought to control accounting techniques and even the methods used by merchants to pay for purchases. Charles VII promulgated royal laws, beginning in 1438, dictating that accounting was to be conducted in **money of account**—either in *Tournois* or *Parisis* silver coinage—and not in real coins.

Requiring accounting to be in money of account was to rely on the stability of royal coinage. In years of strong coinage, that is, with coins of high precious metal content in circulation, calculations in money of account resulted in payment in such coins. This was a seller's or creditor's market. The king was a winner if taxes were paid in coins of good precious metal content. But in a year of weak coinage, buyers and debtors paid in coins of low precious metal content. Periodically, the king chose an alternate tactic. Time and again throughout the Middle Ages the king reduced the precious metal content of coins while keeping the same denomination. At each new minting the king called in all existing coins; then he circulated newly minted royal coins as the only legitimate tender. The king could make precious metal reserves stretch further and gain profit through the remunerative reminting process. He lost in collections of taxes, however, as people paid in the newly debased coins. Monetary deflation plagued royal coinage through the early decades of the fifteenth century, but by 1436 things had improved. Coeur had a role in creating a more positive monetary situation. His appointment by the king to positions of financial authority reflects royal reliance on non-noble technicians and businessmen rather than on the nobility to govern the kingdom.

Hand in hand with official financial functions went Coeur's private financial engagements. Because of his minting experience, Coeur was undoubtedly familiar with practices of monetary exchange (*cambium*) and the profits to be made therein. He acquired a changer's table at the Pont–au–Change in Paris in 1441 and figured in the list of changers in the accounts of the Sainte-Chapelle of Paris, though there is no evidence that he actually practiced the profession of money changer, a prestigious occupation in the Middle Ages, involving some banking operations. The changer's table could simply have been an investment or an avenue that Coeur never had time to pursue fully. He was undoubtedly aware that the practice of exchange was often part of Italian and southern French merchant/banking operations. The Italian companies of the fourteenth and fifteenth centuries were heavily involved in foreign exchange transactions as a means of moving capital around in the interests of commercial affairs but also in regard to financial speculation. The rates of exchange of coinage varied from financial market to financial market across Europe. Merchants attempted to anticipate the rise or decline of certain coinages and to capitalize on changes through timely exchange transactions. Speculation is a part of any monetary economy, and the Middle Ages were no exception.

From the early fourteenth century in Italy and from the later fourteenth century in southern France, exchange transactions had ceased to be recorded by notaries in notarial registers as instruments of exchange and were handled much more freely in so-called "letters of exchange." Messengers or merchants carried these from the market where they were drafted and where credit was initially extended to the market where debts were to be paid off. This system permitted merchants to cope with the need for credit in the perpetual coin shortages of the Middle Ages. It also facilitated business deals among the many different coinages of medieval Europe. But the portable letters of exchange would not necessarily have been recorded or retained by Coeur or any other merchant in a permanent fashion, and thus no such letters are extant for Coeur. In fact, none were available for scrutiny by Jean Dauvet during his examination of Coeur's financial records in the 1450s.

While Coeur was active in minting and advising the king on the first of a series of monetary reforms in the late 1430s (others coming in 1443 and 1451), he embarked upon what was his most famous role, that of *argentier*, best described as a kind of commission agent or bursar from which most of his other activities would henceforth flow. He had distinguished himself in the area of finance, and the king undoubtedly saw in Coeur a talent he needed. At about the age of 40, Coeur began his association with the *Argenterie*, the stores or royal commissary of the king of France, with which his name would be linked forevermore. The fifteenth-century royal counselor and bishop of Lisieux Thomas Basin said it best: "There was in the offices of the king an industrious and shrewd man. . . . He was the *argentier* of the king."[4] Coeur started as a clerk in 1438 at the *Argenterie* and rose rapidly to become *argentier* in 1439. He was named to this office by the king and sworn in by the **Chamber of Accounts**. He also managed the royal stables, which were associated with the *Argenterie*.

Medieval Europe was made up primarily of monarchies, and in a kingdom such as France, the royal administration had been attracting talented men from the non-noble ranks of the bourgeoisie since at least the twelfth century. The French monarchy crafted an alliance

---

[4] Basin, II: 151; Mollat, 31.

with the towns of the realm that strengthened its hand against the nobility. Equally important was the talent pool among urban inhabitants who were trained more practically than the nobility in trade, finance, and law, in the latter case at the new universities emerging in the thirteenth century. To construct his kingdom the king needed men with these talents. Then, too, townsmen and non-nobles, who owed their advancement to royal favor and often their later ennoblement to the king, developed a fierce loyalty to the monarchy, defending and expanding royal interests in a fashion more royalist than the king. They (including Jacques Coeur) thought of these royal interests as their own. The career of Jean II Juvénal des Ursins (1388–1473) illustrates a pattern of success in office that characterized the new nobility, far-removed from the old warrior nobility. From legal positions such as lawyer at the Poitiers *Parlement* (high court), Juvénal became bishop of Beauvais and finally archbishop of Reims. Coeur, from mercantile origins, with his primary incarnation that of *argentier*, also exemplified this new breed of commoner, later ennobled in royal service after serving in multiple official royal capacities in the course of his career. These newly promoted commoners, lawyers and merchants, were still very vulnerable in the fifteenth century to accusations of social climbing and to the envy of the older nobility. Coeur experienced the negative consequences of this remarkable promotion in an equally dramatic fall from grace.

After Coeur's condemnation in 1453, Jean Dauvet inventoried the goods in stock at the *Argenterie* in his efforts to collect the 100,000 *écus* Coeur was judged to owe the king, as well as the 300,000 *écus* in fines assessed against him. The merchandise that Dauvet discovered when he visited the *Argenterie* reveals the nature of Coeur's business as *argentier*.[5] While there is no record of the inventory of stock when Coeur started his career there in the late

---

[5] The historian Michel Mollat studied the 68 folios of the Dauvet journal relating to the *Argenterie* inventory in great detail. Some additional information on the inventory comes from debts owed Jacques Coeur and from papers that were returned to his sons Ravand and Geoffrey at the time of their efforts to rehabilitate Jacques' name and legacy in the 1460s. The statistics given here are taken from Mollat's treatment of the *Argenterie* in Chapter 1, 31–52 of *Jacques Coeur ou l'esprit d'entreprise* (Paris: Aubier, 1988). See also the statistical analysis of the Dauvet inventory done by Mollat et al. in *Marchands et Métiers au Moyen Age*, fascicule 6009 of the collection *Documentation française* (1974).

1430s, and thus his specific contribution cannot be fully evaluated, the data from 1453, meticulously noted by Dauvet in his journal, are evocative of the rich life style of the royal court of Charles VII.

The commissary that the *Argenterie* represented was run as a service to the royal court, though the clientele was broader than the simple circle surrounding the king, his wife, and his children. The *Argenterie* moved with the court in order to be able to supply it, until Coeur established it at a permanent location in Tours. The royal court included members of the royal household and high-ranking officials who administered domestic functions for the king. There were also servants in large numbers, hangers-on, and entertainers. The extended royal family had access to the king's court. Charles VII had a royal favorite, Agnès Sorel, who also maintained a household. Charles inherited the administrative apparatus of the duke of Berry in Bourges. The royal Council, the **Chancery**, or writing office, and the Chamber of Accounts were installed in Bourges. At Poitiers in western France, Charles had his *Parlement* or high court, and a **Cour des Aides** which supervised taxation, that is, in French royal terms, *finances extraordinaries*, as opposed to *finances ordinaries* connected with the traditional revenues attached to the monarchy's estates. Later, even after the recovery of Paris from the English in 1436, Charles VII remained in western central France and had his royal council located at Tours. Armagnac officers predominated in the court of Charles VII. These were loyal supporters, among them the Juvénal family, of which several sons became friends of Jacques Coeur. Personnel in all these capacities could be clients of the *Argenterie*.

With the *Argenterie* under his administration, and with this very large clientele to serve, Coeur functioned, in a military analogy, as a kind of supply officer or bursar for products in demand in royal and noble circles. He was the chief buyer or merchandiser of the royal entourage. A controller oversaw his activities, and both Coeur and this official reported to the Chamber of Accounts. The activities of the *Argenterie* fell into two categories: ordinary or everyday supply, and supply for extraordinary occasions such as royal events, ceremonies, and royal spectacles such as the triumphal entry of Charles VII into Rouen in 1449 after his reconquest of that Norman city from the English. Coeur was himself in the company of the king and other nobles in that royal entry.

The *Argenterie* was like a bazaar or a department store that catered to the tastes of the wealthy of Coeur's time. In 1453 there was merchandise worth about 24,000 *écus* (36,000 *l. t.*).[6] In 1451, the great Florentine merchant banking company of the Medici had a capitalization of 75,000 **florins** (88,750 *l. t.*) In comparative terms, the *Argenterie* merchandise was thus worth more than one third of the Medici bank capitalization at the time the goods were confiscated by Dauvet. Jewels and jewelry accounted for about a fourth of this value. Crosses, necklaces, rings, sequins, and spangles abounded. Gems were present in quantity: sapphires, diamonds, and rubies, among others, as well as pearls. Beyond the jewels, there were gold and silver dishes of many sorts.

The *Argenterie* also featured cloth in pieces of varying size. There were, in all, more than 550 pieces of silk and almost 450 of wool cloth, with an additional 23 pieces of linen and 54 unidentified pieces of cloth. There was cloth of gold and silver, there were velvets of great value and brilliant color such as vermilion, satins with *fleurs de lys* decoration (the French royal emblem of the lily), damasks, taffetas of Florence or Bologna, and silk of various kinds. There were silks of Florentine confection; Coeur himself owned a silk shop in Florence and was a member of the silk corporation. Wool cloth came from Bourges, Lille, Rouen, and Dinan in white, black, or gray. There was already cloth from England in 1453, signaling the end of Hundred Years War hostilities.[7] Reds of various hues predominated in fabric color, present in 95 pieces of wool cloth, 130 of silk, and one of canvas. Blues were slightly more represented than greens, and yellows were a minority, represented only in silk. The great merchants of Italy and southern France at times had shops, but it is unlikely they could tout an inventory this large. Coeur's mercantile background in Bourges prepared him to be well versed in cloth merchandise. For his own attire, Coeur seems to have fancied reds and blacks. (See Author's Preface.)

The *Argenterie* inventory counted some 6,500 pieces of fur and skins of various types, and two hundred coats. These included lamb skins from Aurillac in south-central France and

---

[6] In 1450 the *écu* was worth about 30 *s. t.* and twenty shillings (*sous*) equaled one pound (*livre*). The florin was worth 25 *s. t.* in 1450.

[7] English cloth was undoubtedly absent in 1438–1439, when Coeur took charge.

from Lombardy in northern Italy, along with deerskins. There were furs of squirrel, marten, white fox, ermine, and sable. Some of these furs came from suppliers in the north, from regions around the Baltic Sea, for example. Given Pierre Coeur's occupation as a furrier, Jacques was particularly well qualified to judge good quality merchandise.

Beyond the jewels, luxury fabrics, and furs with which one would expect to outfit a royal court and the nobility, other products were present in the *Argenterie* stores that appealed to a wealthy clientele: chests, inkwells, slates, ivory combs, pitchers, and drinking cups. Since the royal stables and the *Argenterie* were jointly administered, the inventory featured harnesses, game bags, and dog collars. The stables also supplied horses. Coeur was a source of arms to the king of France for his war effort, and it may be in that context that the 1453 inventory recorded a shield from Turkey. He furnished the products and accessories in fashion in Charles VII's France from the *Argenterie* stores.

If the products sold by the *Argenterie* have left considerable trace in the sources, the business operations are difficult to reconstruct in the absence of complete records. The *Argenterie* served as the base of Coeur's operations, from which he orchestrated a geographically dispersed network of agencies. (Chapter 4.) Some few accounts have survived. Additional information comes from the inquests of the legal procedure against Coeur resulting in charges and accusations during his trial, the documents and testimony of Coeur, summoned for his defense, the journal of Jean Dauvet's confiscation efforts, and finally, information assembled in the rehabilitation efforts by his sons, particularly, Archbishop Jean Coeur of Bourges, under King Louis XI in 1462. The *Argenterie* received funds from the royal treasury (**Recettes Générales**), and its operations have left some trace there. The initial capital to fuel the trade necessary for the procurement of products to sell presumably came directly from the king. How the profits were accounted for, once the goods had been sold to Coeur's clientele, is unknown. Theoretically, there should have been an accounting in the Chamber of Accounts. Both the *argentier* and the controller were to submit their accounts to this body. Royal officials had been required to justify their accounts at the royal court since the thirteenth century.

Further, the relationship of the *Argenterie* operations to Coeur's personal finances cannot be untangled. The failure of Coeur's account books to survive makes reconstruction of Coeur's financial operations impossible. His accounts, along with a significant proportion of his mobile wealth, may have been spirited out of France by family and loyal associates to avoid confiscation after the 1453 condemnation decree. When questioned about his records, Coeur stated to Jean Dauvet that he wrote all he knew about his affairs on two pages, perhaps a record of monies owed and owing and no more. This was not enough to satisfy Dauvet, particularly since Coeur's associates could not or would not furnish accounts to him. But Coeur had no reason to assist Dauvet or inform him fully. In one instance, an underling testified that Coeur kept only informal records without specific dates and with rounded figures, again not unusual, but frustrating for Dauvet.[8] With the accounts missing this claim cannot be substantiated, and it is unlikely that an underling was privy to all dimensions of Coeur's accounts. Rounded figures without dates may have served the cause of necessary business confidentiality. Other evidence suggests Coeur kept close control over all aspects of his affairs, as demonstrated below. Moreover, there is no reason to suppose Coeur was unfamiliar with the rather sophisticated written accounting practices that had emerged by his era in Europe.

Double-entry bookkeeping made its appearance in the late thirteenth century in Italy among international merchants. Essentially, there were two entries made, the record of the receipt of goods and either the exit of funds or the record of a debt of equal value, and a record of receipt of funds or money due and a sale of goods of equal value. Another way of looking at double-entry bookkeeping is to think in terms of money out or owed/goods in and goods out/money in or due. The large Italian companies of the fourteenth and fifteenth centuries have left account books that reveal sophisticated accounting systems. None of this is available in Coeur's case as the records have not survived, but had they, there is likelihood that double-entry methods would be found. The two pages written by Coeur for Dauvet imply a balance sheet with assets in terms of cash, receivables, and inventory (goods in) on the one hand, and li-

---

[8] Dauvet, II, 445 (f. 363). See also Michel Mollat, "Une équipe."

abilities in terms of monies owed and profit or loss on sales (goods out) on the other, the profit or loss creating a "balance" between the assets and other liabilities.

The limited surviving documents suggest that Coeur kept track of small details and attempted to pay his debts. In a brief note of 3 January 1444, written at Angers, to merchants of Tours, Coeur stated that these merchants had received for him from a horse merchant the sum of 80 *écus*. Coeur asked the merchants of Tours to pay 100 *écus* to the carrier of this note, a sum that Coeur had promised him, and to put the 20 *écus* outstanding on Coeur's account. He was using these merchants of Tours to clear one debt of 100 *écus* by advancing him some additional funds (20 *écus*) to do this. Without payment of the first sum to the bearer of the note, whose identity is not disclosed, Coeur stated he would be dishonored. These were small sums to a highly placed royal officer, but he dealt personally with their payment. At the top of the letter Coeur appended a brief message to the effect that he wished to speak with these merchants of Tours and would they come to him one day. Coeur confronted the problems of cash flow daily, in terms familiar to all medieval merchants. The medieval economy operated on credit, which reached ever greater dimensions as the volume and size of transactions increased and mint output failed to keep up with the demand for coins because of shortages of precious metals.

Coeur had lines of credit with many of the individuals who were associated with him in one way or another in business. He paid off these debts from time to time. It is often not possible to determine whether official royal or personal engagements were involved in his payments. As a case in point, Coeur corresponded with an unnamed party in a fragmentary document regarding the mother of Charles VII's mistress, Agnès Sorel; 100 *écus* were to be given to her by a merchant of Bourges, Pierre Jobert, one of Coeur's factors, and if Jobert could not furnish the 100 *écus*, then another of Coeur's men was to do so. She was to be told that Coeur authorized up to 300 *francs*, implying a line of credit. There was no pretext given for 100 *écus* payment in the remaining document, dated 2 August 1447. Perhaps the king ordered this on Agnès' request. That Agnès Sorel, who in 1444 became the royal favorite of Charles VII, was associated with the Bourges/Berry faction at court may have prompted Coeur's involvement in resolving this situation.

On the other side of the balance sheet, the debts owed the *Argenterie* for merchandise purchased are staggering. In the mid-fifteenth century Coeur's clientele extended far beyond the royal family, including some 238 debtors from the royal entourage, the nobility, high and low, major office holders, ecclesiastics, and merchants. The *Argenterie* offered convenient access to luxury products that were much in demand. There were no department stores in the period, and products of exotic origin were not easy for individuals to obtain. Clients normally made purchases on credit from the stocks of inventory, and Coeur allowed purchases without credit limits, seemingly, for some clients. The indebtedness of the late medieval nobility is a truism, but within the ranks of *Argenterie* debtors it reached impressive heights. Some nobles had no self-discipline and were focused on maintaining a certain appearance at any cost. Prégent de Coëtivy, the lord of Taillebourg and admiral of France, owed 8,000 *l.* to Coeur but had accumulated debts of 42,000 *l.* from a variety of sources in 1450; this sum surpassed the value of all the *Argenterie* goods in 1453 and represented over half of the Medici capitalization at about the same date. Charles, count of Maine, brother of King René of Anjou, owed the *Argenterie* more than 20,000 *l.*, primarily for luxury fabrics, and in 1456, when Dauvet required him to pay his debts, some of them were more than ten years old. The debts of the count of Maine represented 20 percent of all the outstanding accounts receivable. Though Coeur may not have wanted to carry this level of individual debt for *Argenterie* clients, he was unwilling, out of consideration for King René, or unable to cut off purchasing power because of Charles' position as a member of the high nobility of France, someone a man like Coeur had to treat with respect. It is noteworthy that the indebtedness of *Argenterie* clients might diminish in proportion to the total volume of business of the *Argenterie*, were that to be known.

The case of the count of Maine reveals that he, like many *Argenterie* clients, had a line of credit for purchases, which were then paid for by the assignment to the *Argenterie* of sums due him from the revenues related to his territorial title. Many of the nobility of France had titles like the count's that carried with them extensive lands. The lands in turn were the source of annual tax revenues, which functioned as collateral or could be directed to a creditor. For the nobility land was the primary source of wealth in the Middle Ages, but land often generated a fixed income that was very vulnerable to inflation and fluctuation of coinage values. Given noble tastes, it was common to find the nobility indebted. The level of indebtedness of Coeur's clients at the *Argenterie* was symptomatic of financial problems of the nobility overall in Europe. The indebtedness of *Argenterie* clients may have caused a problem of cash flow for Coeur, causing him to seek additional funding from the king, to carry royal and other debts. Since it was wartime, royal surpluses were non-existent, however, and Coeur probably turned elsewhere to sources of funds that he handled in other capacities for the king. (See below and Chapters 4 and 5.)

Outside the *Argenterie* debts Coeur had other debtors: powerful nobles at the French court, including the queen of France, Marie d'Anjou, and also European royalty such as René d'Anjou, ruler of Provence and king of Sicily. Coeur lent a significant sum to the heir to the throne of Aragon. The indebtedness to Coeur among members of the high nobility of France contributed to his downfall. The king himself was the greatest among these. Charles VII did not set a good example for his extravagant court.

It is impossible to determine the commissions on sales that Coeur himself derived from *Argenterie* operations, presuming he worked on commission rather than on salary. The *Argenterie* was not an ordinary store. The question of profits, if any, is a thorny one. One cannot sort out what was the king's share and what was Coeur's, presuming one can divide things up in this fashion. The historian Jacques Heers has argued that Coeur had funds paid to his personal account that should have been entered at the *Argenterie* or the royal treasury. Some skimming of funds is probably characteristic of many a commission agent, and Coeur would have been the rule, not the exception. Heers also had doubts about the profitability of Coeur's trade, which was the main source of *Argenterie* goods. Heers chose to characterize Coeur as a royal functionary and not a merchant. In contrast, Chapter 4 will present arguments for the success of Coeur's trade. Mediterranean galleys were the mainstay of the shipping empire Coeur established. They supplied many of the oriental luxury fabrics and spices to the *Argenterie* and its clientele. Nonetheless, it remains unknown how Coeur paid for these goods and deducted expenses for their procurement and transport. Moreover, for the integrated system that Coeur orchestrated to supply the *Argenterie*, there was a huge personnel sustaining the enterprise. At some point he had to compensate them for their work, though evidence indicates that he was at times in arrears in the payment of his employees. Coeur's relationship with the *Argenterie* remains cloudy. Perhaps he had a private operation with the *Argenterie* as his client, stemming from the commercial partnership established in 1430 with Pierre Godard and his brother. Coeur may have sold himself goods as merchant to *argentier*. His public and private roles, illustrated by the *Argenterie* operations themselves, invited a comingling of funds that gave him an advantage in the capitalization of his personal business ventures in comparison to the typical medieval merchant operating from his private funds alone. For the time he was in office as *argentier*, from 1439 to his arrest in 1451, Coeur was very good at his job.

In addition to royal mint service, involvement in royal financial policy, and duties at the *Argenterie*, in 1440 Coeur took on additional responsibilities for the king as royal commissioner in Languedoc and Auvergne and served again in that capacity in 1443 and often thereafter. Royal commissioners represented the interests of the king before provincial assemblies such as the Estates of Languedoc and argued the royal case for funding in the form of taxation. As royal commissioner Coeur negotiated on behalf of Charles VII for financial support in the Hundred Years War from the representative assembly of the south of France, the Estates of Languedoc, established at the time in Montpellier. One of his most significant contributions to the war effort of Charles VII was the rationalizing of royal taxation, making it more efficient and more profitable for the king. Coeur's effectiveness in the south of France may have stemmed from the connections he had made earlier in Montpellier during his 1432 Levant trip. In turn his official duties and his commercial interests caused him to set up a site of operations in the Languedocian city. (See Chapter 4.)

The Estates of Languedoc provided a source of cash in the form of subsidies for the king's war efforts. These funds passed through Coeur's hands once he was involved as royal commissioner in the subsidy negotiations. An enterprising official like Coeur might use these to capitalize commercial enterprises whose profits could then fund the king's needs. The absence of Coeur's accounts and Coeur's close control of all aspects of his business complicate the tracking of the sources of funding and the fate of the funds themselves. Then too, Coeur was not interested in oversight by royal officials or by lawyers and investigators, and he undoubtedly understood the usefulness of confidentiality in business.

Whatever the ambiguities in Coeur's business practices, he enjoyed royal favor and considerable success in his early career. By 1440 his increasing responsibility in royal finance, evidenced through his continuing mint responsibilities and his advisory role in monetary policy, his rapid promotion by 1339 to *argentier*, and his designation as royal commissioner in the south of France, testify to his accomplishments and bespeak a man of great talent. His success as royal commissioner led to the expansion of his official roles. Coeur took on the responsibilities of salt tax inspector and tax collector, a vital function in light of the king's military needs. (See Chapter 5.) Jacques Coeur and his family were ennobled by the king in 1441. Charles VII clearly recognized his worth.

Coeur, as a man of the European medieval merchant class, looked at noble status as an ideal. When he was ennobled along with his wife and children, he entered the growing ranks of individuals in France who would attribute their nobility to office and wealth, rather than to blood and military distinction. The king created this nobility of office. Cases such as that of Coeur foreshadow what would come to be called the nobility of the robe (*noblesse de robe*) of the early modern period, opposed to the nobility of the sword (*noblesse d'épée*) or the traditional, hereditary, blood nobility. Writers of the ninth through the eleventh centuries described medieval society as tripartite, composed of those who fought (the nobility), those who prayed (the ecclesiastics), and those who worked (the peasantry). The configuration of society would change over time. Merchants and townspeople were originally marginal to these traditional groups within medieval society, but gradually mercantile activities acquired legitimacy, if not outright respect. However, ennobled merchants retained a certain stigma in the eyes of the traditional nobility and a definite vulnerability, should there be provocation for punishment.

From the later Middle Ages, at least from the reign of Philip IV (1285–1314), it was not uncommon for individuals of bourgeois origin to become members of the royal council, which was the main advisory organ of government surrounding the king, made up traditionally of nobles and high clergy, with the later addition of commoners. Having emerged from the royal court in the thirteenth century, along with the *Parlement* and, slightly later, the Chamber of Accounts, the royal council was a flexible governing body that included those individuals from whom the king sought advice on how to govern. The difficult beginnings of Charles VII certainly encouraged close relations between the bourgeoisie of central France and the monarchy. The Coeur family and their milieu participated in this association. Coeur's case was therefore far from unique in this period of late medieval French history that recorded the upward mobility of numerous urban bourgeois to the rank of noble. However, he reached greater heights than most of his rank. After having been ennobled, along with his family in 1441, Coeur rose even higher in 1442 as he would become a member of the royal council. Such a promotion gave him direct access to the king. Coeur experienced some difficulties in the early years of his career, but there is no doubt but that he made a spectacular beginning. It is time to examine the heyday of Coeur's accomplishments in the decade of the 1440s, beginning with his Mediterranean trading empire.

IV

Commercial Success (1440s)

The decade of the 1440s brought Jacques Coeur to the pinnacle of power. His remarkable success had several dimensions: a vast commercial enterprise (this chapter); financial and diplomatic exploits (Chapter 5); and the creation of a real estate fortune, capped by the construction of his palace in Bourges (Chapter 6). Coeur solidified his position in the royal administration in France in the 1440s by concentrating on trade in the service of the king and on his own behalf. The king was in need of profits from Coeur's trade to further his war efforts against England; Charles VII and his court were also desirous of the luxury products trade could furnish. Coeur used his tremendous talents to satisfy the king's needs and to fulfill his own goal of accumulating personal wealth. The energy and enthusiasm he poured into his commercial ventures also suggest he loved the process of making money, like entrepreneurs of any age. Any attempt to separate royal from personal business in Coeur's activities will fail, and such separation is perhaps anachronistic. In Coeur's case official responsibilities and his own individual actions were intertwined. One must keep in mind that this was an age when there was no clear distinction between the budget of the royal household and the budget of the kingdom, a situation that would plague France well into the eighteenth century.

As *argentier*, Coeur realized that the supply of products of the Mediterranean world to the *Argenterie* and, more broadly, to northern France was in the hands of intermediaries, primarily Italians and, to a lesser degree, southern French merchants. He was determined to eliminate middlemen in the provisioning of French markets with the luxury products of the eastern Mediterranean, South Asia, and the Orient by carving out a role for the direct acquisition of these goods in Levant markets by the French. (See maps on pages 13 and 24.) In this effort to acquire spices, in particular, he set a precedent that would be followed by later French merchants in the service of the state. Coeur brought to this task the experience of his maritime voyage of 1432 to the Levant. He applied the same strategy of eliminating intermediaries in the acquisition of goods from northern Europe for the *Argenterie*, installing his own agents to handle the various stages of importation. To accomplish these ends, Coeur required royal support and royal funds. He needed personnel and the means of transporting goods. He created a remarkable system of agencies run by his people throughout France and beyond, and he made his mark in shipping, particularly in the Mediterranean world, with French ships.

The network of factors and agents that Coeur put in place to handle the business operations of the *Argenterie* and of Mediterranean and Europe-wide trade impressed his contemporaries. The fifteenth-century chroniclers Mathieu d'Escouchy and Georges Chastellain believed that Coeur had 300 factors (commercial agents) on land and on sea.[1] Jean II Juvénal des Ursins (1388–1473), bishop of Laon (later bishop of Beauvais and then archbishop of Reims), author of a chronicle of the reign of Charles VI, and a personal friend of Coeur, remarked: "He has all the merchandise of the realm in his hand and everywhere has his factors."[2] Coeur benefited greatly from his skill in human relations, and in reciprocal fashion, he undoubtedly found friendships in the commercial engagements that brought him fortune. Coeur's early connections with men of his homeland of the Berry represent the nucleus of his business arrangements. The ties forged in these regions sustained Coeur throughout his ca-

---

[1] Mollat, 54 and 402, note 2. D'Escouchy II: 281. See also Michel Mollat, "Une équipe."

[2] Mollat, 53.

reer. Coeur relied in his business on trust, the cornerstone of medieval economic operations. He who was not trustworthy could not achieve great success.

There was an inner circle of individuals, very close to Coeur, who were from Bourges itself. Among these, as noted in Chapter 2, was his boyhood friend and neighbor Guillaume de Varye. Varye, Coeur's premier factor and associate, had a career that closely paralleled Coeur's. He first enjoyed royal favor because his father had lent money to the king. Guillaume de Varye became a clerk of the *Argenterie* in 1438, the same year as Coeur, and was also ennobled in 1441. Fortune followed these promotions. Varye bought a large house in Tours and built a mansion in Bourges. In 1448 he took over the management of the *Argenterie* when Coeur was called to other functions. Varye remained loyal to Coeur during his disgrace. After his arrest, during an interrogation of 26 June 1452, Coeur asked to consult with Varye, as the person who knew his business best, but this request was denied.[3] Varye had, in fact, already left France, traveling in this period to Valencia and Florence. Varye joined Coeur in Rome after his escape from France. Suffering no permanent damage from his association with Coeur, Varye recovered his career under Louis XI, becoming *argentier* for a time. Varye was a talented associate in whom Coeur placed all his trust. What may have distinguished him from Coeur was the latter's self-confidence and optimism, evident in his motto, and the sheer brilliance of the man.

Coeur had other close business associates such as Antoine Noir of Valence and his brothers, who operated from Montpellier to Marseille within Angevin Provence, Avignon (where they had relatives), Lyon, and Geneva, and occasionally as far afield as Barcelona, Rome, and Naples on behalf of Coeur. The Noir brothers joined Coeur in exile in Rome at the end of his life. And, of course, there were the ship captains, Jean de Village, who was also his nephew by marriage, and particularly close to Coeur, Guillaume Gimart, Jean Forest le Jeune, Gaillardet de la Farge, and James Genestet. Later, Jean de Village managed Coeur's affairs in the south of France, in Montpellier, and then in Marseille. He too remained loyal to Coeur and, from his base

---

[3] Guillot, 44.

in Marseille, outside French territory, was instrumental in keeping Coeur's trade functioning during the years of his imprisonment. It was to Jean de Village and Guillaume de Varye that Coeur delegated the most responsibility for his affairs.

Below the associates and major factors (assistants), a broader network of Coeur men radiated out from the core. Coeur's management structure was loosely hierarchical. Every lieutenant or intimate collaborator like Varye had below him other persons, sub-agents, clerks, and servants (all-purpose employees in this case). Servants on salary filled domestic functions but could also be clerks, brokers, or secretaries; they might be involved in packing, handling, and warehousing. It is often difficult to distinguish among these categories. There were factors or business agents who carried out Coeur's directives in agencies across Europe. Coeur used this vast network to assist the king's war effort.

Although the legal ties between these men and Coeur are often obscure or non-existent in the historical record, there is evidence that Coeur established procurations with some of his associates and agents. A common tool of medieval merchants, the **procuration** was a delegation of authority that made the **procurator** a legal representative with a broad or specific mandate to act on behalf of a principal; in Coeur's case, to conduct business at a distance. One of Coeur's procurations survives. In a **contract** dated 1 December 1450, Coeur appointed as procurators his galley skippers and his close collaborators: Jean de Village, Guillaume Gimart, and Antoine Noir, whom he termed his friends and loyal supporters ("*ses amez et feaux*").[4] He accorded them a large mandate to act on his behalf. Each of the three procurators was to act for himself individually and for all collectively. What one did, the others would defend. The procurators could act in court "before all judges, secular and ecclesiastic, commissioners, lieutenants, dispensers of justice, and other officers of whatever power and authority. . . ." These procurators had authority to represent Coeur in real estate matters and to accept in the name of Coeur the legal and physical possession of all offices, lands, lordships, land revenues, possessions, acquisitions and other goods that were his for whatever reason and in

---

[4] Guiraud, Pièces justificatives, VI, 2, pp.144–5, transcribed and reproduced this document.

whatever manner. Coeur gave the procurators an administrative mandate as well: "to order and commit captains, *viguiers* (government officials), provosts, receivers, [tax] farmers, or agents, to remove, exchange, change or move the said officers, farmers or agents; to constrain them to show and exhibit the accounts of receipts and investments they made of money and profits that came and issued from and would come and would issue from the said lands, lordships, possessions and other of the above stated things." Finally, the procuration stated that these representatives had the right to do everything that duly constituted procurators did. In the Middle Ages this was just about anything required by the principals who appointed them as representatives. Coeur delegated broad powers to his closest and most trustworthy men. They could represent him effectively in his absence. As his representatives, they could take a tough stance with underlings.

Communication through correspondence with his associates and factors was one of the means Coeur used to manage his affairs. For example, on 31 December 1450, he wrote to Jean Quercin, whom he styled merchant and guardian of the royal seal in the *bailliage* (administrative district) of Limoges. Quercin functioned as Coeur's factor at Limoges, which was at a crossroads between Tours, where Coeur established the *Argenterie* stores in the later 1440s, and Montpellier in southern France, an important marketplace for products of the Mediterranean world. Quercin had paid for spices, silver, and other merchandise on mandates of payment from Coeur and Coeur's associate, Guillaume de Varye. In his letter, Coeur confirmed that he and Quercin had settled accounts and that he, Coeur, had a remaining credit of 4075 *écus* with Quercin, once an earlier debt of 6075 *écus* was deducted. The failure of the bulk of Coeur's correspondence to survive frustrates efforts to delve deeper into Coeur's business management. As noted earlier, Coeur's men may have sequestered the papers of their master as well as part of his mobile wealth and his accounts after his arrest and spirited these items out of France, perhaps to Marseille.

The business practices just described do not set Coeur apart from most medieval businessmen. However, he was exceptional in the degree to which he traveled to supervise all of his operations. With an extraordinary energy and optimism he directed what happened firsthand whenever possible. Moreover, Coeur had the habit of summoning his associates and employees to his presence, presumably with their paperwork for him to examine for the purposes of accounting; he then transmitted instructions, and they exchanged information. As he expanded his operations in the 1440s, he acquired and built houses spread across France: at Bourges and Tours in central France, and in the south at Montpellier, Marseille, and Lyon, among other cities, to accommodate his peripatetic lifestyle. While none were as lavish as the surviving palace in Bourges, where he could entertain on a par with the nobility, perhaps even the royalty of France (explored in Chapter 6), many were undoubtedly hospitable places where Coeur could receive his friends and associates well. One of his factors, Pierre Jobert, who supervised the building of the palace, along with another bourgeois of Bourges, stated that Coeur could not reside in Bourges permanently or, for that matter, anywhere because of the preoccupations of his own business and that of the king.[5] Face to face, Coeur could lift the morale of his troops and encourage them to complete their tasks. His motto was after all: "For the valiant of heart, nothing is impossible."

As far as actual financial techniques were concerned, Coeur did business mostly through obligatory notes and mandates of payment and with lines of credit. Jean Dauvet preserved traces of these methods and modes of payment in his journal. The trust between Coeur and his associates must have resembled the bond Coeur felt he had with the king. As far as his associates were concerned, Coeur was bound to them by reason of geographic and social origin, family ties, and close cooperation that inspired loyalty. The long-term association between Coeur and his men, who worked for him for many years, encouraged the development of personal ties and even friendships. Jean de Village may have been only 15 years old when he began his association with Coeur. He married Coeur's niece and remained with Coeur the rest of his life. He was also an employee/associate and, in all likelihood, a true friend, perhaps with a filial relationship to Jacques. Although, in some cases, money may have been the foundation of Coeur's connections, these bonds were put to the test after his arrest and condemnation. In the end many friends and associates re-

---

[5] Mollat, 325.

mained loyal to him. (See Chapter 7.) Characteristic of business in the Middle Ages, Coeur's system of operation had a very personal tone, but here too the charismatic Coeur excelled in the degree of loyalty he was able to inspire in the people around him.

Keeping in mind his goal to eliminate intermediaries between the Middle Eastern sources of luxury products and French markets, Coeur crafted a dense network of personnel. He also developed the means of transportation to purchase goods directly in their markets of origin or as close to these as possible. These tactics explain the wide distribution of his agencies and the operations of his agents. Jean de Village, Guillaume Gimart, Antoine Noir, and others sailed the Mediterranean on Coeur's behalf. They were to buy luxury products from South Asia or the Orient in Near Eastern markets through Muslim intermediaries rather than in Europe from Italian merchants. Coeur chose the port of Alexandria in which to concentrate his Levant activities, and his galleys made frequent visits there. He had been there in 1432 and knew the local markets. (See map on p. 23.) Coeur was a master of cross-cultural interaction, soliciting the good will of the sultan of Egypt with diplomatic gifts. Because of the ambivalence of westerners vis-à-vis Islam, these would be misinterpreted at the time of his trial.

Throughout Europe, north and south, he used the same approach to European products that he wished to acquire directly. (See map on p. 13.) Branches and agents were an extension of his own activities. In the north of France he had contacts in Rouen who provided a link with the British Isles on one hand and Flanders on the other. He established a branch of operations in Bruges in Flanders because of the importance of that city in trade and finance in this era. From these northern sources he received cloth and furs, so much in demand in the fifteenth century. In central France, Bourges provided cloth and precious metalwork, and cloth also came from the region of Limoges. At Tours and at Bourges Coeur himself was involved in the production of arms with Italian associates. His arms production should undoubtedly be linked to Charles VII's war effort; then too, significant profits could be made in armaments manufacture in wartime. In Genoa, where he represented the king of France in ambassadorial functions, Coeur also acquired arms. In Florence he had many commercial dealings, joining the formal organization of the Florentine silk guild, the *Arte della Seta*, in 1446, when he decided to produce silks himself in his own silk shop in that city. In eastern France, at Lyon, Coeur concentrated other operations directed to the acquisition of silk, precious metalwork, and rugs. In the south of France, Coeur had establishments in the fair towns of Beaucaire and Pézenas and at Béziers for the acquisition of products of Languedoc such as cloth. Finally, he set up operations in Montpellier and Marseille, both of which were positioned for participation in the Mediterranean trade for which Coeur is famous, that is, in the import of goods such as spices and silks coming from the eastern and western basins of the Mediterranean world— the Near East, including his Levant operation at Alexandria, the Maghreb (the north African coast of what is today Morocco and Tunisia), Italy, and Spain—for marketing in French and northern European venues. For the Mediterranean he needed ships.

Ships and shipping were, in fact, the cornerstone of Coeur's enterprise and the basis of French Mediterranean trade. He opted for galleys. The galley, a common type of Mediterranean ship used in trade and in maritime military activities, was driven by oars that could be supplemented with sails. It had relatively limited cargo space because of the presence of oarsmen. Commercial, as opposed to military, galleys were ships of modest dimensions, forty to fifty meters long and five to six meters wide, with oars and masts for sails, carrying cargoes of maybe 150–200 tons. The *nef*, a rounder, wider ship without oars, also used in Mediterranean trade, carried maybe 1000 tons of cargo. Because of the space limitations of galleys, they tended to carry high-value cargoes such as spices. The luxury products Coeur sought were more costly than bulky.

The evidence suggests that Coeur had, at a minimum, seven ships in the 1440s and 1450s, four of them certainly galleys, an impressive number in this era. A witness in the legal proceedings against Coeur after his arrest in 1451, one Janosso Bucelli, originally of Florence, and at the time of his testimony, a consul of the town **consulate** of Montpellier, testified that Jacques Coeur had at least seven ships.[6] Four galleys were mentioned by Jean Dauvet, in his journal regarding the confiscation and sale of Coeur's fortune after the 1453 condemnation;

---

[6] Mollat, 118.

these were the *Saint–Denis*, the *Saint–Jacques*, the *Saint–Michel*, and the *Madeleine*. The term *Notre–Dame* was at times attached to these ships as in *Notre–Dame–Saint–Jacques*.

Coeur's association with ships began early in the 1440s. In 1443, the galley *Notre–Dame–Saint–Denis* was commissioned by order of King Charles VII from the shipbuilding facilities of the maritime port of Genoa, a site of considerable medieval ship construction. Coeur was made responsible in 1444 for arming and equipping it. This ship was in service in 1445 when it put in at Marseille and took on board several merchants in search of spices. The king's ship, as any other, filled its cargo holds with the merchandise of private parties if there was remaining space. Then, in 1446, Coeur bought, perhaps through an intermediary in Marseille, a galley, the *Notre–Dame–Sainte–Madeleine*, that had belonged to the Hospitallers of Rhodes. Michel Teinturier of Montpellier was its first skipper. Both ships left Marseille in 1446 for the Levant with some Marseillais merchants on board. By 1447 or 1448 the *Notre–Dame–Saint–Jacques* and the *Notre–Dame–Saint–Michel* were also part of the fleet, but their provenance is unknown. By 1447, Jean de Village had replaced Michel Teinturier, who would later be an enemy of Coeur, as skipper of the *Madeleine*. Guillaume Gimart commanded the *Notre–Dame–Saint–Michel*, Jean Forest the Younger and Gaillardet de Boursa the remaining two galleys.

In addition to these four Mediterranean galleys, the names of two other ships have survived: the *Santa–Maria–e–Sant Jacme*, (not to be confused with the *Notre–Dame–Saint–Jacques*) and the *Rose*, also called the "ship of France" ("*navire de France*"). French cultural historian Christian de Mérindol recently linked the choice of names of Coeur's ships to saints and symbols associated with King Charles VII of France, perhaps suggestive of the close relationship between king and *argentier*. The *Rose* was under construction in 1450 and still unfinished in 1451; it is not known whether it was ever completed. The *Santa–Maria–e–Sant–Jacme* was built at Collioure in collaboration with merchants of Roussillon and Catalonia, territories that were part of the kingdom of Aragon at this time. This ship was apparently designed for Atlantic travel and may not have been a galley, as there is a record of its projected voyage to Flanders from Aigues-Mortes, the French royal port near Montpellier that Coeur used for his international trade. There was at least one other ship, the seventh, which can be documented, but its name has not survived. Some of the ships escaped the king's seizure after Coeur's condemnation in 1453 and are only sparsely documented, making it difficult to be certain of the total number. There could have been more than seven, but there were at least seven.

The planning, the time, and the effort that went into the construction of a Mediterranean trading system were Coeur's. However, it is difficult to determine whether Coeur was trading on his own behalf or as a commission agent of the king. Most likely he did both. He may have skimmed profits here as he probably did at the *Argenterie*. And he undoubtedly placed his own merchandise in the galleys along with merchandise to export on the king's behalf. He certainly allowed independent merchants to travel on these ships. Coeur probably filled any vacuum on board his ships with paying merchants' goods and with goods traded on his own behalf. According to the surviving evidence Coeur never skippered his ships, nor did he sail with them; however, the skippers operated under Coeur's orders. But there remains uncertainty regarding whose ships these were in fact.

The historian Jacques Heers maintained that the galleys functioned as official ships of the French state, much as the *Argenterie* served as an official royal commissary. According to Heers, Coeur operated these ships as a kind of royal company or an office of state. He stated, "As for the *Argenterie*, he [Coeur] called upon men of the center of France, principally from his region of the Berry and thus created another clientele of collaborators as faithful, as closely controlled. From this point of view, nothing distinguished the two enterprises, the boutique of the *Argenterie* and the galleys of France, one and the other offices of State."[7] Heers further asserted that these ships were built or acquired with royal funds and sailed as French ships, not ships of Coeur.

In regard to at least some of the ships, the king assisted Coeur financially in acquiring or constructing them. In a brief letter written on 26 July 1451, just before his arrest, Coeur made an acquittal acknowledging to a Master Etienne Petit, treasurer and receiver general

---

[7] Heers, 100.

of Languedoc, his receipt of the sum of 3591 *l. t.* from Charles VII at Taillebourg on 22 July 1451, in addition to other sums also given him, to assist in the construction of a large galley and for matters of ship maintenance.[8] This royal contribution may have supported the on-going construction of the *Rose*. It may have been for another ship altogether. In this acquittal Coeur called himself counselor and *argentier* of the king. In all, Charles VII provided as much as 15,600 *l. t.* to support ship construction from current taxation. Given the wartime demands on royal finances, Coeur must have been extraordinarily persuasive regarding the benefits the king would derive from his maritime investments. After the 29 May 1453 condemnation of Coeur, Jean Dauvet confiscated the ships, once he could sequester them, just as he had confiscated the goods of the *Argenterie* to pay off debts owed to the king by judgment against Coeur. Thereafter, Charles VII briefly chartered the *Madeleine* for a merchant of Béziers; the *Madeleine* ultimately fell into the hands of the Angevins. He had the remaining galleys sold to a merchant named Bernard de Vaulx for a miserable sum compared to what they had cost to purchase or construct. One galley was by then in poor repair.

That the king paid for some ship construction and had the ships confiscated after Coeur's condemnation did not prevent French scholars of southern France and Mediterranean trade, Louise Guiraud and Jean Combes, from considering the ships part of a fleet at Coeur's personal disposal. In her study written 100 years ago, the Montpelliéraine Louise Guiraud took issue with the assessment of Jacques Coeur as an innovator in the commerce of Montpellier because she was aware that southern French merchants had participated in Mediterranean trade for centuries, but she never doubted that he controlled the ships. His captains, many from the Berry and Bourges, sailed them. For Jean Combes, a mid-twentieth-century specialist of Montpellier's commerce, Coeur's fleet represented a more ambitious enterprise than the trade of southern French merchants as it far outstripped the southern French shipping of his day. Combes found the extent of trade in the south of France in the late fourteenth and early fifteenth centuries to be rather modest, due in part to the fact that in the small ports nearest Montpellier there were at best one or two ships in-

---

[8] Mollat, Annexes 3. X, 388.

volved in international commerce, making an annual Mediterranean voyage. Coeur's fleet of seven ships was substantial when viewed comparatively in a southern French context, though in a Mediterranean arena, Venetian and Genoese fleets of galleys and *nefs* were much greater in number of vessels and total tonnage than Coeur's fleet. For Combes, however, to control the means of Mediterranean transportation was a mark of Coeur's originality in the French context and, clearly, a sign of his success.

Coeur had the ships sail proudly with the colors of France, as a Frenchman loyal to his king. He even flew French colors on the ship built at Collioure, though his Catalan collaborators owed loyalties to the Aragonese king. This gesture angered some of these collaborators, and in 1447 Catalans seized the *Santa–Maria–e–Sant–Jacme* en route from Aigues-Mortes to Flanders, an incident that would later become the pretext for one of Coeur's reimbursements for damages via the law of marque. (See Chapter 5.) Coeur was compensated for the ship's seizure. This is direct evidence of independent maritime operations by Coeur.

Coeur's installation in Marseille also bespeaks independent action. Coeur's establishment of Jean de Village in Marseille, his use of that port, and his transfer of the center of his Mediterranean operations to a non-French site suggest that Coeur was working on his own as well as for the king. As early as four months after his arrest and imprisonment in July 1451, the four Mediterranean galleys found refuge in the port of Marseille and benefited from safe-conducts for trade in the ports of Alfonso V (1416–1458), king of Aragon. In 1452 Pope Nicholas V authorized the four galleys to visit and trade freely in territories of the Church. Coeur enjoyed papal privileges to trade with the infidel and to transport persons and goods throughout the Mediterranean world. (See below.) Three of these galleys, under the authority of Jean de Village, Jean Forest, and Gaillardet de Boursa, sailed in the western Mediterranean basin on behalf of Coeur's business, while he was in prison. The fourth, under Guillaume Gimart, traveled to the island of Rhodes in the eastern Mediterranean.[9] Even historian Jacques Heers had to admit that the

---

[9] The legal authority for these operations may have stemmed from the procuration or delegation of legal authority of 1 December 1450 by Coeur to his associates, examined above in the context of Coeur's business entourage.

profits from these voyages were registered to the account of Jean de Village in Marseille and hence to Jacques Coeur.

The question of whose ships Coeur used, whether they were his or the king's, raises the same sort of issues as does the operation of the *Argenterie*; in this, Jacques Heers was correct. But in the case of the galleys and of the *Argenterie*, the question may be anachronistic, reflecting a modern historian's desire for clarity of ownership. Ownership was an illusive idea in the Middle Ages. Possession was a more powerful concept. Many people of the fifteenth century perceived the ships as Coeur's, though they might also assimilate them with the king's business. The king and Coeur shared in the profits derived from the trading enterprise.

The Mediterranean perspective of Coeur's ships was predominant in his maritime activities. Statistically, thanks to Michel Mollat, we can trace about 60 voyages of his ships overall. Approximately half were directed to the Levant, 5 to the Maghreb, about 20 to western Mediterranean Christian shores, and seven to the Atlantic waters between the Bay of Biscay, the French Atlantic and Channel coasts, Bruges, England, and Scotland. Coeur may have eschewed overland transport because of the difficulties caused by the war and opted instead for the Atlantic sea route to northern Europe. The markets of Bruges permitted him to procure necessary northern products—cloth and furs—that joined Mediterranean luxuries, spices, and fabrics sold out of the *Argenterie*. Northern wool cloth was a major European export in the Mediterranean world.

Once he controlled the necessary ships to trade within the Mediterranean world, Coeur still had tremendous challenges before him: To bring the affairs of the king of France and the northern French into fruitful contact with Mediterranean maritime culture. He had a full plate transforming the men of the Berry into sailors, as in the case of Jean de Village, who became captain of the *Notre–Dame–Sainte–Madeleine*, and was established on Coeur's behalf in Marseille. Guillaume Gimart, who captained the *Notre–Dame–Saint–Michel*, was also from the Berry as were Jean Forest the Younger and Gaillardet de Boursa, associated with two other galleys. Then too, the personnel aboard, scribes, officers, and servants, often came from the Berry. Many of these men were related by blood or by marriage. Guillaume Gimart married Jacques Coeur's cousin, Jeanne Heymar, and counted another relative, Jehan de Bourges from the Berry, among the ship personnel. To bind his men to him, Coeur was active in aiding them financially. In a brief note of 22 May 1451 Coeur wrote to Gimart that he would make good on his promise of 1000 *écus* on the occasion of Gimart's marriage.[10] In addition, Coeur asked that whatever expenses Gimart incurred for the clothing of his wife be charged against Coeur's account. Coeur stated further that he would settle up at the end of their association or partnership. These examples could be multiplied. Coeur had southern European collaborators as well, but the flood of men from his homeland who followed him in his Mediterranean maritime adventures remains remarkable. In the course of a decade Coeur created the vast system he had in place at the time of his arrest in 1451.

Even before the acquisition of the first galley, the *Notre–Dame–Saint–Denis* in 1443, Jacques Coeur was preparing connections and facilities in the south of France for a Mediterranean trading presence. About 1440, when Coeur took up the responsibilities of royal commissioner in Languedoc, he again established contacts with merchants of Montpellier, renewing acquaintances from 1432, and began to insert himself into the business community of the town. There were important foreign merchants, Catalans and Italians for the most part, resident in Montpellier, some of them actual immigrants. There were Jews in the town as well. These groups were benefiting from the promised tax relief accorded by the town consuls.

Although the medieval heyday of Montpellier in commerce and finance lay well in the past, having peaked by 1350, beyond the merchant community per se, several urban industries continued to function in the 1430s and 1440s. Cloth dyeing, which had brought the town renown in the twelfth and thirteenth centuries, still existed. There were workshops producing gold work, enamels, and fine knives. Remnants of the earlier banking industry were still present as well. In the hinterland, the production of wine, olive oil, and wool dominated the rural economy.

Coeur, as a royal commissioner sent by the king of France to the Estates of Languedoc to obtain subsidies for royal expenses,

---

[10] Mollat, Annexes 3. IX, 387.

had reason to frequent Montpellier. He also served as inspector general for the salt tax in the south in the 1440s. (See Chapter 5.) Additionally, he acquired the farm of the prestigious Languedocian fairs of Pézenas and Montagnac, from which he derived revenues relating to fair sales and activities. From 1440 to 1445, the town of Montpellier paid him a retainer of 250 *écus* in order to benefit from his protection and favorable dealings in regard to tax burdens, as he was by now a powerful influence in royal circles. These connections in Montpellier and in Languedoc provided Coeur with a springboard for his maritime ambitions.

The physical features of local geography guided the commercial system that Coeur established. The coast of lower Languedoc near Montpellier was not well endowed with ports. Lattes, the traditional port of Montpellier, was actually located on an inland waterway or lagoon, the Etang de Pérols, and not on the Mediterranean coast itself. Lattes was connected by a road with the town of Montpellier. From the sea one reached Lattes in small boats into which cargo had been transferred from Mediterranean vessels. Goods then made their way to the markets of Montpellier in carts overland. The great natural harbor of Marseille far outstripped ports in Languedoc, but Marseille lay outside French territory in Provence. Until he moved his operations to Marseille, Coeur needed a viable port for international trade near Montpellier.

The French royal port of Aigues-Mortes, about 25 kilometers from Montpellier, linked to Lattes by another lagoon (the Etang de Mauguio) and a canal system, served Coeur's ends. Aigues-Mortes had been built in the thirteenth century and was the port from which Saint Louis sailed on his first crusade in 1248. It was situated several kilometers inland from the sea and connected to the Mediterranean by canals that had the perennial tendency to sand and silt up. Lacking a favorable natural environment, in the fourteenth and fifteenth centuries the inhabitants of the area faced a constant struggle and considerable expense to keep open the access of Aigues-Mortes to the sea and to the inland waterway. Equally problematic was the absence of natural shelter for ships exposed to pirates and weather as they anchored offshore for the downloading of cargo. However, because it was the only French royal port on the Mediterranean, Aigues-Mortes had benefited from royal monopolies since the late thirteenth century. In 1278, Philip III of France had decreed that all Italians living in Montpellier move to Nîmes and that goods enter the south of France via the port of Aigues-Mortes and proceed to Nîmes. This proved an unsuccessful attempt on the part of the French to squeeze Montpellier, then a Majorcan enclave in French territory, out of Mediterranean trade.

A century and a half later it was at Aigues-Mortes and at Montpellier that Jacques Coeur first concentrated his southern French commercial operations. Coeur viewed the proximity of Nîmes as an advantage, with its access to the Rhône River valley corridor for the transport of goods. Coeur encouraged the repair of the port of Aigues-Mortes and contributed to its revival through the construction of a canal connecting the port with the Rhône River. All was not smooth sailing, however. Coeur came into conflict with the local interests of Montpellier as early as 1442, when he disagreed with the town consuls over the choice of treasurer for Aigues-Mortes. He sought to prevent the nomination of Pierre Teinturier by the consuls, because he wanted open trade, in opposition to control by local influence, a move that contributed to the alienation of this Montpellier family, who would later figure among his enemies at the time of his arrest. For the time being, Coeur would prevail, and both Michel and Pierre Teinturier would serve him as galley captains in the 1440s. In 1444, Coeur installed his shipyards at Aigues-Mortes, and it was from there in the mid-1440s that the French fleet made its entrance into the world of Mediterranean commerce in search of spices, in particular.

The spice trade had, for a millenium and more, dominated the luxury trade of Europeans, who were always seeking new sources and easier access to supplies. Spices meant almost anything coming from the lands of the Indian Ocean, the Spice Islands, and the South China Sea that could be used as medicine, as a dye for cloth, or to season food. Such goods were called by medieval merchants "*avoir du poids*," which meant literally "to have weight" but figuratively signaled value. Spices familiar to the modern kitchen were always the most important: pepper, cinnamon, and cloves.[11] From the Middle Ages on, Europeans were accustomed to using rather

---

[11] Spices can be distinguished from herbs in that they are something hard, a seed or a bark, as opposed to herbs such as parsley, sage, and rosemary, which are leaves.

large quantities of these spices. Spices were believed to have a salutary medicinal effect. They were used to flavor foods and also could serve as food perservatives. Within medieval society, spices were a status symbol because of their high cost.

From an early era, the search was on to gain access to spice supplies. In the thirteenth century Genoese and Venetian merchants such as Marco Polo traveled east across Asia in search of spices. By the fifteenth century, Spanish and Portuguese of the Iberian Peninsula, blocked by the Italians, especially the Venetians, from access to the spice markets of the eastern Mediterranean, were increasingly motivated to seek faster, shorter, more direct routes to the sources of spices via the Atlantic Ocean and beyond. The gold trade in Africa also attracted the attention of these merchants and explorers. Europe was in need of gold to finance the purchase of luxury goods in eastern Mediterranean markets. There had always been an outflow of precious metals from Europe to the east as a function of the imbalance of trade. The late fourteenth century ushered in an era of conspicious consumption heightening the demand for luxuries such as spices. European population declined dramatically in the plagues of the fourteenth century; the Black Death of 1348–1352 claimed between a fourth and a third of the population as a whole, and subsequent visitations of the plague took additional victims. The survivors enjoyed more resources because of their fewer numbers, and a rising standard of living was the result.

In the 1440s for Coeur and the French, the horizons of the spice trade stopped in the Levant. Despite their Atlantic coastline, the French were drawn to the Mediterranean world. Coeur sought only to eliminate intermediaries for the French in the Mediterranean spice trade. Moreover, exploration in the footsteps of the Spanish and the Portuguese was not yet cost-effective for an *argentier*, and was never a consideration; war financing took precedence. Coeur's major competitors were the Venetians and the Genoese and, to a much lesser degree, the Catalans of the Crown of Aragon. However, the Ottoman empire, with its base in Turkey, was creating some difficulties of supply for the markets serving Europeans in the Near East. Coeur was obliged to utilize Near Eastern markets that were in more friendly Muslim lands, working through Egypt and the markets of Alexandria.

By 1445 Coeur had obtained from the king of France a tax advantage on spice imports through Aigues-Mortes, which were free of duty for him here, though taxed at ten percent of their value at every other port. Of all branches within the Mediterranean luxury trade, spices were the particular focus of Coeur's own operations. Moreover, thanks to the king of France, Coeur would have the right to conscript oarsmen forcibly to man his galleys, a first in northern French Mediterranean experience. The trading advantages Coeur enjoyed were poorly received by his competitors, who viewed his privileges as a monopoly, particularly in regard to the spice trade. A legal proceeding of the Council of Barcelona of 11 August 1449 stated: "It was exposed in the present Council that the *argentier* of the king of France had two galleys at sea and that, in order to prohibit other persons from bringing spices to France, and in order to reserve the profits to his galleys, he provoked the imposition by the king of France of a tax of ten percent on all the spices that would be imported, unless through the port of Aigues-Mortes which is reserved for the *argentier*, in such a way that France, which used to get its provisions in spices in this principality (Catalonia) and especially in this city (Barcelona), now receives neither large or small quantities."[12] Public opinion held that the French royal port of Aigues-Mortes, in which Coeur encouraged Charles VII to invest heavily, was reserved for his trade, according to monopolies granted by the French king. It was later maintained that the ten percent tax from which Coeur's galleys were exempt had ruined the Catalan commerce in spices. Another complaint implied that all merchandise imported into France from Catalonia was taxed.

At the same time that Coeur was having the French fleet constructed and was restoring the port of Aigues-Mortes, he was positioning himself in the Mediterranean world through French royal diplomacy in support of maritime trade. In 1445, Coeur facilitated the conclusion of a treaty between the sultan of Egypt and the Knights of Rhodes that may have served both French and papal interests. Using his royal and personal connections through his brother Nicolas, a highly placed member of the Church, Coeur received permission from

---

[12] Marinesco, Nouveaux, 168-9.

the pope in 1446 to trade for five years with the infidel. The port of Alexandria to which he directed his trade was a Muslim port, and he was in need of official dispensation. In 1447 Jean de Village, representing Coeur, established on behalf of the king of France a political and commercial alliance with the sultan of Egypt. The pope renewed Coeur's privileges of trade with the infidel in 1448 and extended them for Coeur's lifetime, also giving him the right to transport pilgrims to the Holy Land and Muslims throughout the Mediterranean. Such favors greatly enhanced Coeur's Mediterranean trading ventures, which in turn served French royal interests in stocking the *Argenterie* with desirable merchandise and in furthering the trade in spices. Coeur's cross-cultural engagements reflect the expanding, yet highly ambivalent, relationship of Europe with the Islamic world, particularly in regard to the foreign trade that was assuming greater proportions for Europe, and for France, in particular, in the transitional fifteenth century.

Coeur served his king through the performance of royal duties but also saw to his own commercial interests. In fact, these privileges, along with the possession of a fleet of galleys, gave Coeur the possibility of transporting not only his own goods and goods destined for the *Argenterie* but those of other merchants as well. Once imported goods were in France, Coeur managed overland transport services, with his own carts driven by his own transporters frequenting the route from Montpellier to the *Argenterie* in Tours, to Paris, and to Bruges.

To further his trading enterprise Jacques Coeur carried out some of his most innovative real estate ventures, notably in the construction of a commercial exchange, the *Grande-Loge*, at Montpellier. At the end of the fourteenth century, letters of John, duke of Berry, who succeeded his brother, Louis of Anjou, as lieutenant of the king in Languedoc, and of King Charles VI (1380–1422) confirm the existence of an earlier exchange or *loge*, later called the *Petite-Loge*, which the pepperers of Montpellier had been instrumental in constructing to further their trade in spices. When Coeur established his Mediterranean operations at Montpellier, he decided to construct a commercial exchange in the town on a par with those in Perpignan, Barcelona, Palma de Majorca, Genoa, Venice, Gaëta, Naples, Palermo, and even Rhodes. The exchange was to be a gathering place for merchants, where contacts were made, deals crafted, and information and news shared. Coeur persuaded the town of

Montpellier to participate in the construction of this *loge* by allocating a reduction of royal taxes (the *tailles*), beginning in 1445. Coeur had the authority as a royal commissioner to the Estates of Languedoc to make concessions of this sort, which reinforced his widely perceived and legitimate power. Coeur was convinced that his trade and the king's would be enhanced with a commercial exchange. Moreover, the king's revenues were underwriting the venture. Montpellier and its merchants should have profited.

Coeur acquired land near Notre–Dame–des–Tables, the pilgrimage church in Montpellier around which the money changers with their tables had early established themselves. This was prime commercial terrain in the market center of the old town of Montpellier. With Coeur's backing the exchange was completed in less than a year. The result was a two-story rectangular building with a terrace at the top, facing the Place des Changes across from Notre–Dame–des–Tables. In one corner was an octagonal tower housing the staircase. The building was adorned with Coeur's arms, those of the town of Montpellier, and a stag with a royal banner, a symbol of King Charles VII.[13]

Coeur remained in contact with Montpellier and the exchange in the years 1446–1449 and continued to invest in the town. Beyond the *loge*, he had three other properties in Montpellier, two large houses and a stable. He was also associated with the construction of a fountain called the Font Putanelle in the suburbs of Montpellier in 1447. On this structure were emblazoned the arms of Coeur and those of Montpellier. Coeur's interest in providing the town with a fountain may have been less to see to the needs of the urban population of this semi-arid region than to assist in the production of a dyeing facility that he had intended to build in Montpellier to revive the scarlet dyeing trade, famous earlier in the Middle Ages. Though construction of the *loge* in Montpellier had gone quickly, in 1453–1457, at the time of the confiscations of Jean Dauvet, there were still unpaid accounts relating to both the fountain and the exchange. After Coeur's condemnation, attempts to auction off the exchange in 1454 were unsuccessful.

---

[13] The *loge* does not survive today in its medieval form, though parts of it are incorporated into the Hôtel de Lunaret, which is the current site of the Museum of Languedoc, sponsored by the Société Archéologique de Montpellier.

Even as Coeur was constructing the Montpellier *loge*, he was developing his commercial activities at Marseille in Provence from the mid-1440s. Provence was not within the political sway of the French king at this time but in the direct possession of the Angevins, a dynasty descended from its thirteenth-century founder, Charles of Anjou, younger brother of Saint Louis (1226–1270). Provence in the first half of the fifteenth century, under the Angevin descendant Good King René, a brother-in-law of the king of France, was a kingdom, independent in its own right, which would not come under the domination of the kings of France until 1481 during the reign of Louis XI. (See Chapters 5 and 7 on King René.) The port of Marseille was the best natural port on the Mediterranean coast between Genoa and Barcelona. (See map on p. 23.) Coeur placed Jean de Village in charge of operations in Marseille in the 1440s. He and Jean obtained rights of bourgeoisie in Marseille in the later 1440s. One wonders if Coeur was covering all his bases in the event that his position in France deteriorated. In the end Coeur abandoned Montpellier for the much more desirable Provençal port. This would prove serendipitous, for Marseille would be beyond the reach of the French king's men after Coeur's arrest.

There are no known northern French precedents for the system that Coeur constructed in the Mediterranean world. Thomas Basin, bishop of Lisieux, stated categorically, "It is he, the first of all the French of his time, to equip and arm galleys that, loaded with woolen garments and other products of the workshops of France, traveled up and down the coasts of Africa and the East."[14] If any northern Frenchmen had achieved the prestige that Jacques Coeur was to garner in Mediterranean trade, history would have preserved some trace of them. Coeur's business techniques owed some debt to Italian precedents; he had models for his technical contracts, partnerships, procurations, obligatory notes, mandates of payment, and credit lines in the very competitors he sought to displace. The network of agencies that Coeur spun out from the *Argenterie* across French territory and beyond bears some comparison, geographically, to Italian models, the vast system of branch offices of the great fourteenth-century companies of the Bardi and Peruzzi or the Medici in the fifteenth century. Between 1310 and 1345 the Bardi company of

---

[14] Heers, 85.

Florence had some 346 agents at more than 25 branch offices in Italy, France, England, Spain, the Low Countries, Tunis in North Africa, and as far afield as the Levant. The average employment of a Bardi agent was 11 to 12 years, suggesting that in any one year something over one hundred agents were in Bardi employ. For the Bardi and Peruzzi, operating under a system of unlimited liability, the financial difficulties of one branch were assumed by the company as a whole, and a disaster could and did bring down the entire structure in the 1340s. In the fifteenth century, the Medici of Florence ran the business of their branches independently to avoid the perils of unlimited liability.[15] Geographic expanse still characterized the Medici operations, as it did those of Jacques Coeur.

Coeur's cumulation of public and private roles also finds precedent on the Italian scene. Although the Italian companies were private enterprises, Italian politics allowed for an intermingling of public and private roles. There was no king in northern Italy at this time, though the south of the peninsula had long been incorporated into a Mediterranean kingdom. Rather, there were city states and city republics in the north. It was the merchants of Venice, Genoa, and Florence, in particular, but also of Milan, who set the standard by which mercantile activities have been judged in the Middle Ages. Their home cities were independent of any outside political authority. Merchants of these city states were at times called on to perform as officials. They served in city government and also as ambassadors of their states vis-à-vis the international community. The economic historian Robert S. Lopez spoke of the Italian cities as governments of the merchants, by the merchants, and for the merchants. Elsewhere in other European towns, one can find parallels for the mixing of personal and official roles. That merchants held official roles did not disqualify them as merchants, and there has been no attempt by modern economic historians to view the great merchant houses of Italy as other than commercially oriented. By comparison, Coeur's position in the France of his time

---

[15] It will be recalled that the Medici controlled assets of about 75,000 florins (88,750 *l. t.*) in 1451, with about one-quarter of these invested in two wool shops and one silk shop in Florence. Iron and alum mining and textile manufacture, wool cloth and silks, as well as banking and trade represented Medici company activities. About 22,500 florins (28,100 *l. t.*) in profits were generated from these shops, accounting for 12 percent of the company profits of the years 1441–1451.

was admittedly somewhat unusual, and his combined identity as both merchant and royal official dwarfed any comparable examples among his compatriots. Coeur had significant personal investments, but his role of public renown was that of *argentier*, royal commission agent catering to the needs of the monarchy.

There were also differences between Coeur and Italian models. Operationally, the directors of the great Italian merchant companies traveled only exceptionally; their branch offices represent a managerial innovation of the later thirteenth century. In contrast, Coeur was constantly on the move to oversee his widely dispersed business concerns and to carry out the service of the French king. While Italian companies contracted for many of their needs, hiring outside services and personnel, Coeur controlled the purchase, transport, and marketing of products, particularly of the Levant, within France to a royal and noble clientele. He enjoyed large tax advantages, if not monopoly status, over competitors. The French king provided the source of Coeur's funding for everything from stocking the *Argenterie* to the construction of ships for Mediterranean trade.

If Coeur's enterprise can be usefully compared and contrasted with that of Italian companies, there were few individuals with his high profile. One such, however, was the thirteenth-century Genoese merchant and admiral Benedetto Zaccaria. Zaccaria wore several hats, just as Coeur did. He was admiral, industrialist, and merchant. He was a very wealthy man when he died in 1307 or 1308, combining a monopoly of alum production (a fixative used in dyeing cloth) in Phocaea, worth 50,000 *l.* Genoese a year, plantations of mastic trees that yielded a resinous substance used in varnishes and coatings, and ship ownership. Trade, investments in real estate and public debts, and various salaries and pensions rounded out his fortune. In 1277, Zaccaria sent his galleys to England, participating in the opening of the Atlantic sea route between the Mediterranean and the North Sea. He served more than one master, in 1281 sailing for the king of Castile in attempts to rid the Straits of Gibraltar of Muslim maritime operations. Thanks to Zaccaria's efforts, in the early fourteenth century the Genoese and Venetians added England and the Atlantic passage to the ports of call on the well-defined routes of their convoys of ships. Zaccaria also shared with Coeur an involvement in crusade. Zaccaria ceased a potentially profitable blockade of Sluys and Bruges in the Low Countries to plan a crusade. Zaccaria was able to conduct his business through partnership (*commenda*) investments, one-time commitments of funds from many small investors of Genoa for one commercial venture, and through the use of procurations delegating authority to trusted agents and associates, particularly his brother Manuelo. The business techniques of the thirteenth-century Zaccaria, on a far smaller scale than the complex company partnerships of the Bardi and Peruzzi of the fourteenth century and the Medici of the fifteenth, were still tried and true in the fifteenth-century Mediterranean world that was Coeur's primary arena of activity.

Close scrutiny of the organization of Coeur's enterprise has revealed his management skills and business techniques. The commercial machine Coeur developed was much like an operation of military logistics, an organizational form that was without parallel in business in his era or any preceding period. Coeur convinced Charles VII to finance his commercial vision, even in a time of war. The king contributed to the construction of ships. Coeur then directed his galleys to trade in the Mediterranean, with all the attendant personnel necessary. He planned and acquired funds for the support system, with installations at Montpellier and upgrading of facilities at the port of Aigues-Mortes with royal tax advantages there. He organized overland transport from the coast to inland markets. He directed French diplomacy in the eastern Mediterranean to favor good relations with the sultan of Egypt for access to the port of Alexandria, and he obtained papal blessing for his trade with Muslims. Coeur's career foreshadowed future French development. As Robert Guillot, author of a study of the law suit against Coeur, remarked, "Finally, when he obtained for his galleys the monopoly of importation of spices and of transport of French goods in Muslim ports, Jacques Coeur contributed to the orientation of the commercial politics of the crown towards planned solutions which, from the reign of Louis XI to the French Revolution, would often be imposed on the world of business."[16] One can see the beginnings of early modern mercantilism.

The question of why Coeur directed his efforts single-mindedly to the Mediterranean economic arena and failed to enter into the age of European expansion is not difficult to comprehend when one

---

[16] Guillot, 20.

considers that he was in many ways a traditional medieval merchant, not an explorer like the Portuguese Vasco da Gama. He was a Frenchman of land-locked central France, who embarked on an extraordinary career in Mediterranean trade in the forefront of his compatriots; he was not an adventurer in the early age of European discoveries but rather someone interested in the exploitation of the commercial resources of known lands. In seeking a spice monopoly for the French in the Levant, he foreshadowed later French efforts to gain access to spices in Asia. However, French historians Jean Favier and Edouard Perroy took Coeur to task for not realizing the potential of the wider world of the early fifteenth century. In the end this is not a useful critique as it would take several revolutions of thought before Europeans understood that a wider world lay before them. From the perspective of northern and central France, where the crusade tradition propelled people to journey to distant lands, the Mediterranean remained the source of exotic products.

Although the main focus of Coeur's trade was the Mediterranean arena, he was also engaged in maritime activities outside the Mediterranean. The specific geographic and cartographic knowledge to which Coeur might have been exposed and what he and his collaborators knew of the Atlantic Mediterranean remain intriguing questions. As noted above, Michel Mollat documented seven Atlantic voyages for Coeur's ships. The *Santa–Maria–e–Sant–Jacme*, constructed along with another ship in Collioure, was destined for Atlantic travel. The expected itinerary was that of Mediterranean cogs since the late thirteenth century: around Spain, and up the Atlantic coast of France to the Channel and the North Sea, with Bruges a likely destination of some of the goods. It is possible that Coeur and others in the royal entourage at Bourges had actually seen world maps (*mappaemundi*), taking note of the growing list of discoveries. The duke of Berry had several *mappaemundi* in his collection, though whether they represented current geographic knowledge cannot be determined. Moreover, there is evidence that Jan van Eyck created a *mappamundi* for the duke of Burgundy between 1430 and 1440, at the time the latter sent agents such as Bertrandon de la Broquière to the Levant to gather intelligence for a future crusade. But motives were lacking for exploration and for colonization in the case of Coeur, as he could obtain spices in the Levant through Muslim sources. His Mediterranean perspective remained unchanged by a few voyages of his ships in the Atlantic and North Sea. Moreover, the primary purpose of the Atlantic navigation of Coeur's ships was trade with northern Europe. Coeur did not imitate the Atlantic exploits of the fifteenth-century Genoese, Castilians, and Portuguese nor indeed of those "bold Norman sailors" in the words of Edouard Perroy, who founded an ephemeral Canaries kingdom in the early fifteenth century.[17]

Coeur concentrated the bulk of his operations on the Mediterranean world, and his primary aim was to control international commerce of Near Eastern products. He sought direct French access to the markets of the Levant. To achieve this he was prepared to innovate, to create commercial exchanges like that of Montpellier. Michel Mollat described Jacques Coeur as a first among equals as far as French merchants were concerned, one who revived the central role of French merchants in French trade, which had disappeared with the decline of the Champagne fairs in the first half of the fourteenth century. Coeur's aims for personal gain paralleled his official responsibility to turn a profit to assist the king financially in the challenges of the Hundred Years War. These choices make him a complex figure to evaluate in terms of the dichotomy of "medieval" versus "transitional." To understand Coeur it is necessary to acknowledge that he utilized the commercial opportunities and techniques available to him and suitable to his ends. In his methods he harked back to the thirteenth century and looked forward to the mercantilism of the *Ancien Régime*. The trading system constructed by Jacques Coeur to supply the needs of the monarchy and those of clients of the *Argenterie* and to build his own fortune is perhaps the most striking achievement of Coeur's heyday of power in the 1440s. The profits he generated financed the king's military undertakings and contributed to the French victory in the Hundred Years War. He himself became a very wealthy man. It is time to consider the financial dimensions of Coeur's official roles and entrepreneurship.

---

[17] Edouard Perroy, *The Hundred Years War* (New York: Capricorn Books, 1965), 327.

Finance and
Diplomacy (1440s)

Commercial success represents the first dimension of Coeur's career at its height. Finance and diplomacy, often closely intertwined, comprise a second aspect, also centered in that key decade of his heyday, the 1440s. Financial demands fell heavily on Jacques Coeur. Coeur's responsibility to assist the military operations of Charles VII monetarily in the reconquest of French territory from the English and the need to extend credit to a cash-poor nobility and royalty, his clients for the goods of the *Argenterie*, caused him to speculate at the highest level of European finance. Cash flow was a constant problem for Coeur. He engaged in a wide variety of financial operations, facilitated undoubtedly by the technical expertise he had acquired in his early years. He advised the king in monetary policy that led to the adjustment of the royal coinage in France, he procured tax revenues from Languedoc and promoted the royal salt tax, he attempted to rejuvenate the exploitation of metal mines in the Lyonnais and Beaujolais, and he sought the import of metal objects to feed the royal mints. In terms of international finance, Coeur engaged in diplomacy in the area of Mediterranean reprisals for piracy and derived revenues from decisions according to the law of marque. To further his trade and royal trade, he obtained diplomatic concessions from kings and popes. In these ventures he made much by way of personal profit but directed large sums to the king's military needs as well. His exploits caused Coeur to be characterized as a royal financier, analogous to a finance minister, though the term is anachronistic for the period; for some he was the greatest financier of the fifteenth century.[1]

Coeur's many fiscal and administrative initiatives contributed to significant achievements for the French monarchy in the last decades of the Hundred Years War, that is, permanent taxation and a standing army. By 1440 direct taxation through the *taille* (tallage on households and hearths) had been made permanent, as had indirect taxation in the form of a tax of 1/12 on merchandise. These gains in permanent taxation permitted the establishment of a reliable armed force. Beginning in 1445, the king laid the groundwork for a standing army which would amount to approximately 25,000 men in arms by the end of the fifteenth century (noted in the Introduction), the largest and most effective fighting force in Europe at that time.

It is possible to reconstruct, at least partially, the involvement of Jacques Coeur in royal finance; his contribution went far beyond his roles at the *Argenterie* and in Mediterranean and European trade. Coeur was responsible for funding a sizeable portion of the king's military operations in the war against the English. The fifteenth-century chronicler Mathieu d'Escouchy recounted how Jacques Coeur advanced the king money for the Normandy campaign in 1449–1450, in the amount of 200,000 *écus*.[2] Coeur may have borrowed from Italian bankers or from French sources, and he could have utilized tax revenues from Languedoc to assemble this sum. On 12 December 1450, Coeur wrote an acquittal for the repayment to him of a loan made for the military operations to free Cherbourg in Normandy, which was occupied by the English, whom Coeur called "ancient enemies of this kingdom."[3] Identifying himself as counselor and *argentier* of the king, he acknowledged receiving from Macé de Lannoy, the receiver general of finances for Normandy, the sum of 60,000 *l. t.*, paid by the receiver general as reimbursement for a loan by Coeur to the king in August for the liberation of Cherbourg. Coeur held himself content and well paid and quit of the

---

[1] See Heers, 46–7, for a discussion of nineteenth-century misnomers of Coeur's responsibilities.

[2] Heers, 146; Mollat, 228.

[3] Mollat, Annexes 3. VII, 385: "les Angloiz, anciens ennemis de ce royaume."

king, de Lannoy, and all others to whom the acquittal was due. He signed this letter with a seal depicting his personal coat of arms. How Coeur acquired the funds for the loan is unknown.

War finance created problems of cash flow. On 10 March 1450, Coeur wrote to the duchess of Burgundy, Isabella of Portugal, about the 4000 *l. t.* of tax receipts from the northern French province of Vermandois that he could not pay on behalf of the king because of heavy expenses in the Normandy campaign: "My very formidable lady, I commend myself the most humbly I can to your good grace." At the end of this missive, Coeur added, "I beg you, my very formidable lady, as humbly as I am able, that it please you to excuse me at this time; but, God willing, in time and place I intend to pursue the matter and others with the king, with my small power, where it will please you to employ me. And always let it please you to inform me and command me to do your very good bidding, to accomplish these, our Lord willing; let him by his grace, my very formidable lady, grant you a very good life."[4] Coeur took a polite, even submissive tone, to convey the distasteful message of non-payment, but with a very legitimate excuse—the cash flow problems stemming from the needs of war finance.

In order to raise the thousands necessary for the French war effort, Coeur reformed royal salt production and taxation. From the fourteenth century, the French monarchy had asserted its control over the production of salt, the sale of which it taxed. In the growing arsenal of French taxes the salt tax (*gabelle*) represented one of the most fruitful because of salt's role as a necessity of life. Salt was produced along the shores of the Mediterranean and was distributed via the Rhône River valley corridor. Atlantic salt was produced from the Bay of Biscay in the south to Brittany in the north. Coeur's specialty was in the manufacture and marketing of salt from Languedoc. He had made inroads in the south of France through his role as royal commissioner in 1440 in Languedoc and Auvergne, serving again in that capacity in 1443 and often thereafter. To these responsibilities he added that of inspector general (*visiteur général*) of the salt taxes (*gabelles)* of Languedoc, the Guyenne, the Lyonnais, and the Mâconnais in the 1440s. (See map on p. 13.) In his official capacity Coeur sent instructions from Montpellier on 13 March 1448 to Humbert

---

[4] Mollat, Annexes 3. VI: 383–4.

Fournier, the royal official (*châtelain*) of Condrieu near Lyon, to the effect that the administrative districts of Lyon and Mâcon were obliged to use Languedocian salt that had been taxed at one of the pay stations of Languedoc.[5] Currently, merchants were bringing in salt from the German Empire, Burgundy, and western France for inhabitants of the Mâconnais and the Lyonnais, causing the king to lose salt tax revenues. Coeur ordered Humbert Fournier to investigate these crimes over the course of a year and to summon the accused before a judicial tribunal in Pont–Saint–Esprit. Coeur's particular target was the Burgundian salt distribution system that had made serious inroads into the French market; he would win a place within France for the salt of the Languedocian littoral that he distributed via the Rhône River corridor.

This traffic was extremely lucrative. Salt warehouses on the Mediterranean coast and on the French side of the Rhône have left records of the *gabelle* tax for the period 1 September 1448 to 31 August 1450 in two yearly levies that yielded 58,000 *l.* and 72,000 *l.* respectively, implying massive salt production. Coeur controlled these sums as inspector general; he seems to have been guilty of some fraud, here as elsewhere, according to the trial testimony of the official in charge of the Pont–Saint–Esprit salt granary, after Coeur's arrest in 1451.[6]

To strengthen his role in the *gabelle* system, Coeur insinuated himself into the bourgeoisie of Lyon, located on the Rhône. In 1446, he was listed in a property register of Lyon as holding six buildings in a wealthy quarter of that town.[7] The register, interestingly, uses the term "valiants" (*vaillants*) to refer to those inhabitants with fortune (perhaps from the term *valoir*, to be worth); Coeur figured in this category. His motto, "For the valiant of heart, nothing is impossible" ("A cuer vaillans, rien impossible"), may thus be a play on words, to be read on several levels: Perhaps for the rich, nothing is impossible, but this may be too crass an interpretation for the fifteenth century. Yet, for someone as enamored with money, fortune, power, and display as Jacques Coeur, the materialistic twist must be retained as a possibility.

---

[5] Mollat, Annexes 3. IV: 380–1.

[6] Mollat, 79–80.

[7] Mollat, 82.

Beyond salt, another area of royal resources in need of Coeur's management was the supply of precious metals to the royal mints. Chapter 3 described Coeur's monetary reform efforts. In the 1440s he became involved in supplying precious metal to the royal mints that were consistently short of raw material, particularly pure metal that could be used to mint good-quality coins. This was a chronic problem of the late Middle Ages. The fifteenth-century monastic chronicler Adrien de But recounted that Jacques Coeur requested from the duke of Burgundy the right to buy precious metal objects in Flanders to increase the monetary supplies of the French mints and, in turn, assist the war effort.[8] France was anything but a major site of gold and silver reserves, and the provisioning of royal mints became a major preoccupation throughout the Middle Ages. Gold was almost absent from western Europe and was traditionally acquired by Europeans trading in north Africa where trans-Saharan gold was available. The major European sources of silver were in the Harz Mountains in Germany, though there were some minor deposits in central, southern, and eastern France. In 1444, in a personal venture, Coeur took on farm—for a tenth of the tax—the royal mines of silver, lead, and copper in the Beaujolais and Lyonnais regions. Later he acquired an interest in their direct exploitation. One of the witnesses in the interrogations of the law suit after Coeur's arrest, Jean Vanerst, stated that Coeur had forbidden him to record the output of the Lyonnais mines.[9] Though such deception could indicate a tendency to defraud, perhaps Coeur gave this order as a wartime strategy to conceal French resources. Coeur also seems to have been interested in Languedocian reserves near the town of Sommières. The return, if any, from these enterprises is unknown. Jean Dauvet made two trips to the mines of the Lyonnais, determining that there was not much to be salvaged for the confiscation effort.

In addition to mining, coinage also offered Coeur challenges and occasioned later accusations. Given the difficulties of provisioning the royal mints in precious metals, export of French coins, precious metal bars, and plate was forbidden. Though

[8] Mollat, 294.

[9] Mollat, 257, called him Vannerot; Heers, 41.

Coeur served as a mint official and as royal financial advisor and made efforts to acquire precious metals for the royal mints, ironically, he was himself accused of the export of precious metal upon his arrest in 1451.

From the late 1430s, in part because of Coeur's role in royal monetary policy and practices in this period, France ceased to be plagued by coinage fluctuations, with fewer mutations of both gold and silver coins. Even after Coeur had ceased to hold mint offices, his influence could be felt via his minions at the Bourges mint and at the Montpellier mint and through the person of Ravand le Danois, Coeur's early associate at the mint of Bourges where Coeur, Ravand, and another were caught in monetary fraud in the late 1420s. Ravand later served at the Montélimar mint in 1445 and thereafter at the Paris mint as general master of mints. Beyond royal service, however, Coeur may have had additional motives for gaining expertise in coinage practices and in the refinement and mixing of precious metals for the purpose of coinage.

Coeur was interested in making money any way he could; he may even have sought to transform base metal into gold. Here, as in all other endeavors, success would have benefited him and the king. Associated with matters of minting and mine exploitation was the medieval fascination with alchemy. The interest in a means to change base metal into precious metal coursed through high and low culture in the Middle Ages. Medieval science held that all matter was made up of four elements: earth, fire, water, and air. Through applications of cooling, heating, wetting, and drying, the so-called "applied physics" of alchemy hoped to purify matter to find the fifth and quintessential element, the philosopher's stone, believed to facilitate the process of conversion of base metal to gold. Echoes of this quest resonate today. The children's literature hero Harry Potter's first challenge was to protect the philosopher's stone. Great medieval thinkers such as Albertus Magnus (1193–1280) engaged in alchemical experimentation in search of this element. While gold was never produced, alcohol and *eau-de-vie* (brandies and liqueurs) were medieval offshoots of alchemical research into the fermenting and distilling processes.

In the late 1430s and 1440s Coeur's duties of policing royal coinage brought him face to face with alchemical practices or rumors thereof. In a letter of 8 April, undated as to the year, to a cer-

tain Monsieur de Barbançoys, perhaps the squire Hélion de Bra-
bançois, lord of Sarzay, Coeur wrote about a man who told him in
secret that the tax official of Saint Benoyst (probably
Saint–Benoît–sur–Loire, a site of royal tax collection), was in contact
with alchemists who were counterfeiting *écus* to pay men of arms
and in one case had exchanged five ingots of alchemical gold for
authentic metal.[10] The informant also recounted that the tax collector and the alchemists met at night and exchanged more ingots
at an inn with the sign of a wild man in Saint–Benoît. Coeur ordered this informant to spy on the tax collector and all those who
came to the inn, and to bring the suspicious parties to Bourges in
order that an inquest might be conducted into these matters. Acting in the general role of royal monetary consultant, Coeur impressed upon the squire, as the authority figure of the area, that
this was a matter of great importance to the king.

The legends that surround Coeur contain the argument that
he was a master alchemist. Building on the belief that his title of
argentier meant silversmith, authors espousing this theory interpret everything from his motto, "For the valiant of heart, nothing is impossible," to decorative details such as a small sculptured relief of Tristan and Isolde with King Mark in the treasure
room of his palace in Bourges in terms of alchemical symbolism.[11] The number of physical details in the Bourges house that
are open to alchemical interpretation suggest, at the least, that
Coeur was caught up in the enthusiasm of his day for alchemy.
There is, however, no evidence that Coeur attempted alchemical
experiments or even patronized such "science." How convenient it would have been for Charles VII's war effort if Jacques
Coeur had been a successful alchemist! To say more, in the current state of research, would be to push the envelope; however,
when one considers that Sir Isaac Newton (1642–1727) may
have been the last great alchemist and that his alchemical writ-
ings appear to have meant more to him than his "orthodox" scientific endeavors, it may be necessary to set aside twenty-first
century skepticism in order to understand the mentality of indi-

---

[10] Mollat, Annexes 3. XI: 389. Coeur called the alchemists "arquemiens."

[11] For example, see Roger Facon and Jean-Marie Parent, *Gilles de Rais et Jacques Coeur. La conspiration des innocents* (Paris: Robert Laffont, 1984).

viduals of earlier eras, even that of the scientific age of Newton-ian physics, to say nothing of those who lived in the period of turmoil and change of the late Middle Ages.

A more realistic arena for gain came again from the Mediter-ranean, in regard to recompense for losses due to piracy or priva-teering. Piracy, rampant in the Mediterranean for centuries, was two-fold. One form of piracy was independent theft on the high seas. The pirate operated on his own, generally targeting merchant ships. Another form was officially sanctioned. The **privateer,** some-times called a **corsair,** had the blessing of a political authority to confiscate the ships of enemies or rivals to avenge some wrong. Reprisals bred more reprisals. The fourteenth century saw the be-ginning of the distinction between pirate and privateer that reached full development in the sixteenth century. The Atlantic world would have its share of both pirates and corsairs in the early modern era, but by the late seventeenth century control over the use of force by the maturing nation states led to a decline in privateering and reprisal. Piracy lived on and still plagues vessels in the modern age.

In the fifteenth century pirates and privateers abounded in the Italian port cities, in the kingdom of Aragon, and among the Greeks and Muslims. The law of marque developed as an area of medieval international law that involved reprisal to indemnify mer-chants whose goods were unjustly seized by pirates or privateers or to permit them to recover monies owed, such as unpaid debts. Vic-tims could appeal to the political authority of the perpetrators' country or region of origin about compensation for an act of mar-itime robbery, but should their requests not be honored, they might address their complaints to their own political authority, often a king, who could accord what was called a **letter of marque,** of which examples survive from as early as the mid-thirteenth century, permitting the victim to seek retribution for his wrong by penalizing compatriots of the perpetrators. This means of redress of wrongs often resulted in additional victims. The original defendants could simply seize the goods and sometimes the persons of innocent resi-dents of the same city as that of the wrongdoers. At sea, this meant that a Frenchman, who had been the victim of, say, a pirate of Ma-jorcan origins, could legally—armed with a letter of marque—force the surrender of any Majorcan ship he might come across, even that of a perfectly innocent merchant. The rationale was to cause collective public pressure on the wrongdoers to make amends. In the late Middle Ages, Christine de Pisan and other authors spoke out against the injustice of letters of marque, which they claimed were little better than a license to prey on others.

By the fifteenth century, perhaps in response to the chaos resulting from the violence of the implementation of marques, reprisals were increasingly transformed into taxation on trade to generate funds to pay compensation to victims and break the cycle of violence. The taxation solution to reprisals required a territorial base for liability; the fiscal/administrative approach spread to a number of lands in the western Mediterranean basin, among them Catalonia, Genoa, Provence, and Avignon, where remedies for crimes under the law of marque were collected as taxes. This bureaucratic approach eliminated the thorny problem of whether one was pirate or privateer/corsair, thus illegal or sanctioned. It was permissible for an enterprising merchant like Coeur to profit through financial speculation by farming the taxes destined as reimbursements. He would also qualify for recompense in the capacity of victim. Coeur had nothing of the pirate about him, but armed reprisals were committed by the captains of his galleys after his arrest in 1451. Where he excelled was in the new diplomatic solution of taxation to provide restitution for piracy.

Coeur inserted himself into the lucrative process of marques in the 1440s, on his own behalf as victim and in an official capacity. The proceeds of marques were paid to three categories of individuals: commissioners who heard and judged the cases of plaintiffs and decided who should be considered victims; tax farmers who bid to collect the tax revenues; and, perhaps last, the victims of piracy themselves. Coeur was involved at all three levels in law of marque operations in the Mediterranean. He participated in the farm of a compensatory tax for Catalonia. Some of the Catalan complaints about his monopoly in the spice trade, aired in Chapter 4, resulted from this tax. He was the farmer of the marque of Genoa, and likely commissioner of the marque of Provence. He was also a victim to be recompensed.

Above and beyond these roles, Coeur was involved in diplomacy among Mediterranean sovereigns over the adjudication of marques and the level of taxation as recompense. He negotiated on behalf of the king of France in lengthy deliberations with the crown of Aragon regarding the marque of Catalonia; in the course of these his assistance was sought in reducing marque exactions. These issues were very important to Coeur because of his commitment to Mediterranean trade on his own behalf and on behalf of the king of France.

As royal advisor and a member of the French royal council, Coeur was a participant in a commission composed of French and Aragonese members that dealt with the marque of Catalonia for a number of years (e.g., 1437–1442) in regard to reprisals in France against Catalan merchants. In 1441 and 1442, marque negotiations led to a tax of 5 pennies per pound (*d./l.*) on merchandise of trade flowing in both directions between France and Aragon, to be collected for the reimbursement of victims. Coeur seems to have profited, along with one of his Catalan associates, Joan Llobera, from the farm of the marque of Catalonia. Parties dissatisfied with the judgments of the commission included merchants of Perpignan, Barcelona, and Montpellier. One issue was the tax imposed on Catalan trade to France to resolve the marque, the collection of which was to extend over five and one-half years. The Council of Barcelona suggested that complaints from Perpignan and Barcelona be directed to the king and queen of Aragon and that French merchants should appeal to Charles VII and the *Parlement de Toulouse*. Queen Maria of Aragon, who was the lieutenant of her husband in Catalonia, asked Jacques Coeur to do away with these taxes. The counselors of Barcelona were concerned that Coeur, as a farmer of this tax, would act only in his own interests. These discussions dragged on. In June 1445 Jacques Coeur arrived in Barcelona on a commercial galley ("*una galea de mercaderia*").[12] While in Catalonia, Coeur discussed the situation with the counselors of Barcelona, agreeing to renounce his rights to this tax, on condition of being reimbursed for damages. The Catalans felt the tax had ruined their trade with France. On his side, Coeur joined the politics of marque to his desire and ambition to further his monopoly on French Mediterranean trade, particularly that in spices.

Coeur had his own early experience of piracy on his 1432 return voyage from the Levant, when ship and passengers were

---

[12] See my discussion of these issues in my paper, "Commercial Law and Merchant Disputes: Jacques Coeur and the Law of Marque," forthcoming in *Medieval Encounters*.

seized by Corsicans. Many years after the fact, this incident led to a classic example of the proceedings of a marque commission with a resolution to reimburse the victims. As noted earlier, the galley in which Coeur was traveling was wrecked off the coast of Corsica near the port of Calvi; a captain of the island and his cohorts illegally seized the travelers and as much of their cargo as they could recover. It may well have been pressure from Coeur, in a position of power in the 1440s, that finally brought this affair to a hearing. On Friday, 2 September 1444, the proceedings addressing this event opened in the reception hall of the Montpellier house of the honorable Jacques de Gaudiaco, judge of the **Petit Scel**, a French court of voluntary juris-diction, *sceaux rigoureux*, specializing in commercial disputes, in the presence of commissioners of the king of Aragon, the governor of Montpellier and the judge of Nîmes, commissioners of the king of France, and judges of the *Petit Scel* and of Béziers. Petitions came from the victims of the Corsicans, including the heirs of Jean Vitalis, late bourgeois of Narbonne, Augustin Siquardi, Jacques and Naude-tus de Proxida, brothers and merchants of Montpellier, Jean Ebreardi of Agde, Jean Brunelli and Pierre Egidii of Montpellier, and Jacques Coeur (*Jacobus Cordis*), merchant of Bourges. The hearing must then have been postponed, perhaps so that the commission could scrutinize the information before it.

In November 1444, when the case once again came before the court, the assembled deliberators had before them much documentation with which to verify the petition. They awarded to the heirs of Jean Vitalis, the ship owner, the sum of 2224 *l.* 15 *s. t.*, taking into account interest on the 800 ducats that had been paid for his release, his detention, and court expenses, and to Augustin Siquardi, the ship's captain, 350 *l.* 10 *s. t.*. Both Vi-talis and Siquardi had been detained and ransomed. Other awards included 180 *l. t.* for the Proxida brothers; 27 *l. t.* for Ebreardi of Agde; 13 *l.* 10 *s. t.* for Brunelli and Egidii; 27 *l. t.* for Jacques Coeur. The commission stated further that it could not judge on the value of the merchandise on board because only one-sixth of it had reached the shore at Calvi, the rest being lost with the ship. Since the inhabitants of Calvi were under Genoese authority, but Corsica was Aragonese, marques against Genoa and Catalonia were presumably to be applied to generate funds to pay the awards of damages.

There are two other incidents involving the law of marque in which Coeur claimed recompense for his losses and those of his son Ravand. In 1444, shortly after the *Notre–Dame–Saint–Denis* was constructed in Genoese shipyards at the order of the king of France, the Genoese captured it in the port of Aigues-Mortes as a result of a complicated diplomatic situation at Genoa in the 1440s, explored further below. In retaliation, goods of the Genoese, then in Aigues-Mortes, were seized. Coeur recovered his ship in November 1445. From testimony associated with Coeur's trial, the slow speed of the indemnification process is evident. Out of a projected collection of 21,000–25,000 *écus* (36,000–37,500 *l. t.*) from the marques of Genoa and Catalonia, spread over 21 years, Coeur was allotted 13,609 *écus* (20,413.5 *l. t.*) in 1446, in recompense for the seizure of the *Notre–Dame–Saint–Denis*. However, after five years Coeur had collected only 2148 *écus* (3222 *l. t.*), about one-sixth of the initial award. In addition, the cooperative farm of these marques brought Jacques Coeur individually about 240 *écus* (360 *l. t.*) a year, a relatively modest sum. Coeur, like all victims, was faced with slow proceedings and partial recompense, even when he was administering them himself.

At Collioure, in the summer of 1447, Catalan merchants, who had collaborated with Coeur in the construction of the *Santa–Maria–e–Sant–Jacme*, destined for Atlantic travel, arrested the ship en route from Aigues-Mortes to Flanders via the Roussillonnais port of Collioure because it was flying the colors of the king of France, an offense to Catalan ego, as noted in Chapter 4. The ship's cargo of wine destined for sale in Flanders was lost as a result of this incident, not because of the delay the detainment caused but rather because the wine barrels were not waterproof and had been improperly stowed on board. Regardless, Coeur claimed compensation.

Coeur certainly manipulated matters in regard to marques, as he did in other areas, using his influence with the royal council and the king. Coeur was concerned with financing the king's war ventures, and he confronted constant cash flow issues. His aim was always the greatest gain. For example, in 1443 he obtained letters from Charles VII on behalf of the citizens of Avignon and the Comtat Venaissin, releasing them from marques adjudged by the *Petit Scel* of Montpellier. For this Coeur received 5000 *écus* from the inhabitants of Avignon for his influence. He later argued that, in accord with decisions of the Estates of Languedoc and the great council of the king of France, this sum was used on behalf of the king; he had kept only 500 *écus* or ten percent. In the case of the marque of Genoa, Coeur was rewarded many times over: first, for his role as victim for the Corsican incident, and then as victim at Aigues-Mortes, via an overestimate of his own damages and a concurrent underestimate of those of other victims, then as marque commissioner, next for his part in the farm of the marque, and, finally, with an augmentation, perhaps unjustified, for the costs of administering the marque. He may have been slow in paying out the proceeds of the marque to other victims, but what he kept for himself did not reach exorbitant levels. Of 7530 *écus* (11,295 *l. t.*) collected from the marque of Genoa, Coeur supposedly got 600 in all, the same amount as several other highly placed individuals but five times less than that of the king of France. In another version of events regarding the adjudication of the marque of Genoa, a trial witness, Secondino Bossavini, one of the participants in the 1432 voyage, testified that Coeur called the victims together and told them that he had incurred great expenses and demanded 6000 *écus*.[13] The victims did not dare contradict him because of his power and authority. Under interrogation, Coeur had to admit that he forced the victims to agree and that the king of France received nothing of the sum. What Coeur did with the money is unknown, but he undoubtedly had many pressing debts.

In regard to the marque of Catalonia, Coeur maintained that he received 6000 *écus* (9000 *l. t.*) through royal agreement and that these were later distributed: 1363 **l. t.** was that of the victims, and 2000 *écus* (3000 *l. t.*) his own recompense because of his personal losses in the galley of Narbonne. He did not account for the remainder of the 6000 *écus*. What he meant by the galley of Narbonne is obscure since his indemnity for his 1432 losses in the galley of Narbonne were adjudged at only 27 *l. t.*, unless he made a later claim for merchandise that was never recovered from the shipwreck. In regard to 12,000 florins (15,000 *l. t.*) from the marque of Provence, Coeur maintained that he received them in the summer of 1449 by authority of the king and had not been able to distribute

---

[13] Mollat, 235–6; Guillot, 52.

them to those who were to be indemnified. Instead he had to rush to rejoin the king, who in the fall of 1449 was embarking on the reconquest of the Guyenne. Here, as in some other instances, Coeur appeared ill-informed, or his testimony was inaccurately recorded. The Normandy campaign occurred in 1449–1450; that of the Guyenne was 1451–1453. However, Coeur's explanation of why he did not reimburse the victims suggests these florins had been incorporated into monies provided to the king for the army. He did meet up with the king on campaign in Normandy. Tens of thousands of *écus* flowed through Coeur's hands from marque judgments and negotiations. Recompensing piracy and privateering was big business.

Marque negotiations occupied only a part of Coeur's diplomatic activities in the 1440s. From the official roles of mint master, *argentier*, and tax official, as his career progressed, Coeur graduated to the position of ambassador and diplomat and represented the king on other royal missions abroad. Coeur's close associate Guillaume de Varye took over management of the *Argenterie* once Coeur became preoccupied with these missions. Coeur's responsibilities involved him in multiple endeavors, often costly affairs, on behalf of the monarchy outside France, in pursuit of royal ambitions. In 1445 and again in 1446 he served as ambassador to Genoa for the French king. Charles VII wished to control Genoa in the tradition of French kings from the end of the fourteenth century. From Montpellier, on 15 February 1447 (n. s.), Coeur wrote about Genoese affairs to royal ambassadors Pierre de Brézé, count of Evreux and grand seneschal of Normandy, and Bertrand de Beauvau, lord of Précigny. Coeur feared but could not believe news of the betrayal of Janus de Campo Fregoso, the ruler who had taken power in Genoa as of 30 January 1447, with the support of the French. Coeur had received letters from the receiver general of finances, Jean Barillet de Xaincoins, reporting on the situation in Genoa. In the letter of 15 February, Coeur used grandiose, figurative language, construing himself as necessary to the realization of the goal of the king of France to rule in Genoa. "I know well that the conquest of the Holy Grail can not happen without me."[14] The Grail quest was a common literary theme of epic and romance in the Middle Ages, but its invocation by Coeur here seems excessive. To

---

[14] Mollat, Annexes 3. II: 377–8.

further the French cause of the moment in Genoa, Coeur wanted the king and his forces to arrive at Lyon, threatening further movement to Italy while he, Coeur, put pressure on contacts in Nice. However difficult negotiations with Genoa were, Coeur often profited. On his own behalf, Coeur and his men were the beneficiaries of numerous safe-conducts in the late 1440s for Mediterranean travel via Genoa.

Within the Mediterranean context, the place of the Aragonese kingdom was especially significant as it controlled most of Spain's Mediterranean coast. In spite of damage done to Catalan trade, particularly in spices, Coeur benefited from many instances of favor at the hands of the king of Aragon and Naples, Alfonso V. At the time of the negotiations regarding marque reprisals for piracy and in regard to protection for his ships that persisted beyond the moments of his arrest (1451) and condemnation (1453), the esteem in which Alfonso held Coeur is striking indeed. In May 1446 Alfonso wrote to Coeur, "You will have occasion to realize that we will always accord a particular attention to you and your affairs and that, when the captains of your galleys wish for safe-conducts, we will accord them with the greatest benevolence, out of esteem for you."[15] Also in May 1446 the queen of France, Marie d'Anjou, thanked the king of Aragon herself for the consideration he had shown Coeur, behavior that Alfonso himself explained through the "esteem and affection" the French sovereigns themselves showed Coeur.[16] This is significant testimony to the favor that Coeur enjoyed at this time from Charles VII of France. Alfonso took his cue from the French monarchs, but his own graciousness toward Coeur would outlast the French king's grace. Alfonso clearly respected Coeur and went out of his way to support his commercial endeavors through access to Catalonian ports and through safe-conducts for his galleys before and after Coeur's arrest. The relations between these two went beyond the simple diplomatic interview; the tie between Alfonso and Coeur has a personal ring in this correspondence. In spite of certain conflicts, which pitted Aragon against France and even Coeur against Aragon in law of marque

---

[15] Mollat, 148. See also Marinesco, "Du nouveau sur Jacques Coeur," and "Nouveaux renseignements sur Jacques Coeur."

[16] Mollat, 148.

settlements, Alfonso remained his supporter. As late as 1455, Alfonso ordered that his safe-conducts to Coeur, in exile in Rome, and to certain of Coeur's men remain valid.

The diplomatic efforts Coeur undertook for the king of France offered him further outlets through which to garner power and connections, notably the possibility of becoming acquainted with churchmen, even with popes. The fourteenth and early fifteenth centuries brought considerable turmoil to the late medieval Church. The election of rival popes after the end of the Avignon papacy (1309–1376) caused what would be termed the Great Schism. The **Council of Constance** (1414–1417) finally resolved the problem of two and sometimes three rival popes with the persistence of just one pope, Martin V, after 1418. But the resolution was short-lived. **Conciliarism** (the belief that ecclesiastical leadership resided in general church councils) at the **Council of Basel** (1431–1449) reintroduced the problem of more than one pope. In 1439, the year Coeur became *argentier*, the Council of Basel forced the legitimate pope, Eugenius IV, to step down and elected, instead, as antipope Felix V (1439–1449), the former duke of Savoy, Amadeus VIII. Charles VII tried to mediate between the council and Pope Eugenius IV, who would live until 1447. Charles called an assembly of French clergy at Bourges, where in 1438 they issued the **Pragmatic Sanction** that reestablished elections for the major ecclesiastical positions in France, with some leniency for papal influence but with no provision for papal intervention in lesser benefices or Church offices. The popes, it will be recalled, had been very supportive of Coeur's efforts to develop French trade. In 1445, Coeur had received permission from the pope to trade for five years with the infidel. In the same year he facilitated a treaty between the Knights of Rhodes and the sultan of Egypt, also noted in Chapter 4. In 1446, the pope authorized a special export of arms as a gift from the king of France to the sultan of Egypt, and in 1447 Jean de Village established a political and commercial alliance with the sultan of Egypt on behalf of the king of France. These alliances served the cause of king and pope but also Jacques Coeur. In 1448, Charles VII invited Coeur to take part in a French embassy to the new pope, Nicholas V (1447–1455), Eugenius' rightful successor, in Rome. Coeur would join a group of participants who had already been active in negotiations to resolve the schism at the Council of Basel.

The French embassy of 1448 was an extravagant undertaking. Coeur worked behind the scenes to choreograph the French efforts with a magnificent parade of 300 horses. He undoubtedly also orchestrated the financing of such extravagance. Most participants returned to France after a month's stay in Rome, but Coeur was taken ill and given hospitality by the pope with treatment by the papal physician. Here was an opportunity for Coeur and Pope Nicholas V to become acquainted. In the long run, this connection benefited Coeur well after his escape from France. (See Chapters 7 and 8.) More immediately, Coeur's privilege of trade with the infidel was renewed in 1448 for his lifetime. He was influential in negotiating, on behalf of the king of France, the abdication of the antipope Felix in 1449, a significant achievement and one for which Pope Nicholas V was very grateful. Nicholas would welcome Coeur in exile in Rome in 1455.

On balance, in the 1440s, Coeur had many strategies to cope with financial needs and the problems of cash flow for himself and his king. Coeur's endeavors in finance were often combined with diplomacy as he did the king's business and his own. He manipulated the coinage along with associates at various mints, siphoned off tax revenues from Languedoc, rejuvenated the exploitation of metal mines in the Lyonnais, and sought the procurement of metal objects to keep the royal mints from closing because of a shortage of precious metal to coin. Coeur's practices are nowhere better illustrated than in the law of marque proceedings. The establishment of order in the Mediterranean through marque reprisals against piracy was very important to the survival and flourishing of Coeur's trade initiatives. Coeur used the revenues garnered through the imposition of the Mediterranean marques of the 1440s to recompense himself as victim of piracy and as commissioner and farmer of the reprisal bureaucracy. From these many sources of revenue he funneled money to Charles VII for campaigns in the Hundred Years War. Coeur rejoiced in royal victories and helped to communicate the good news. There survives a short document of 14 November 1449, noting the payment of 16 *l. t.* to a squire who acted as messenger for Coeur to the Great Council of the king, then at Montpellier, to announce the capture of the city of Rouen in upper Normandy from the English, as well as the towns of Fougères in Brittany, and Arques and Caudebec in Normandy.[17] Coeur accompanied Charles VII in his triumphal entry into Rouen in 1449. He was energetically committed to the king and the king's cause of winning the war. Coeur the royal official and Coeur the merchant and financier are inseparable. One cannot be certain that he made distinctions himself. Bending the rules at times, his conduct was typical of the medieval merchant and royal official, simply on an enlarged scale, given his stature and the cash flow needs of his king and French trade. Contemporary commentators thought him unjustly accused of financial mismanagement. The fifteenth-century chronicler Mathieu d'Escouchy quoted him as stating at one point in the Normandy campaign, "Sire, all I have is yours." ("*Sire, ce que j'ay est vôtre.*")[18] One might add that Coeur felt the reverse was also true. Until he fell victim to strict censure when abandoned by the king, he was able to maintain a lavish lifestyle. It is time to examine what profits could buy and build.

---

[17] Mollat, Annexes 3. V: 382.

[18] D'Escouchy, II: 286; Mollat, 238.

The Fruits of
Enterprise (1440s)

Coeur's commercial, financial, and diplomatic efforts served the king and yielded many advantages for him and his family, including ennoblement (1441) and membership in the royal council (1442). In the same period his brother Nicolas received promotion to the bishopric of Luçon (1441). Coeur's material wealth increased greatly in the decade of the 1440s. Though his possessions multiplied across a broad French geography, it was in Bourges, the Berry, and to a somewhat lesser degree, the Bourbonnais, his father's *pays*, that one finds the greatest concentration. Bourges was always the primary focus of Coeur's allegiance. His attachments in men and landed fortune began there and radiated out. No matter how much he traveled, he would always come back to Bourges. The construction of his palace in Bourges began in 1443. (See photo on p. 10.) With wealth came philanthropy, and the cathedral of Bourges was a beneficiary of Coeur's generosity. In 1445, Coeur financed the construction of a new sacristy at the cathedral, and two years later he had a funerary chapel built for the Coeur family, graced with an extraordinary stained glass window depicting the Annunciation. In 1450, his son Jean became archbishop of Bourges at the age of 26. These are signs that Coeur was rising dramatically within the social and economic hierarchy of France during the 1440s, the era that certainly represented his heyday.

The ways Coeur used his newly acquired wealth are revealing of late medieval society. The most striking offshoot was a drive to possess land, resulting in enhanced personal status. In Europe and in many civilizations of the pre-industrial period, the major source of power was land and real property rights. The nobility and monarchies controlled most of the land. There is no escaping the hold on people's imaginations that monarchy, nobility, and landed fortune exercised. Fortunately, it is possible to reconstruct Coeur's landed wealth from a variety of sources. The survival of his palace in Bourges provides a unique opportunity to observe his lifestyle through his daily surroundings.

Coeur's fortune followed the typical pattern of urban medieval wealth that derived primarily from trade and finance. He was in the unusual position of benefiting, as well, from revenues stemming from royal taxation. Merchant families held land in the urban context from an early date. However, noble estates predominated in the countryside. By the fourteenth and fifteenth centuries, the European nobility had fallen on hard times financially. The old nobility often had their resources invested in fixed revenues from land, traditional rights paid by users at permanent rates that were not adjusted for inflation. Inflationary cycles characterized the late Middle Ages, and devaluation of coinage contributed to the financial dilemma of the nobility. Noble income fell over time, leaving the nobility impoverished but spurred by an ever greater conspicuous consumption, due to the pressures of plague, war, and status. Shaken by the Black Death of the mid-fourteenth century and by repeated outbreaks of the plague, with fears exacerbated by the recurring crises of the Hundred Years War, people were uncertain about the future. They lived extravagantly for the moment. Forced to borrow to support an increasingly lavish lifestyle, the nobility became indebted to wealthy townspeople for luxury goods. Frequently, the latter purchased the rural estates of nobles no longer able to afford them.

Coeur was adept at discovering situations where landholders were forced to sell their lands because of debts. Foreclosures because of debt were common in France from the fourteenth century. Beginning in the late 1430s, Coeur concentrated his acquisitions of land, châteaux, and country houses in the Berry and in the Bourbonnais, with extensions southeast toward the Lyonnais and the Forez and northeast toward the Gâtinais and Champagne. He also acquired at least two rural properties in lower Languedoc. These domains represented primarily noble lands as opposed to lands of commoners. In France land was classified either as noble or non-noble. There was a special category of noble estate originally held by the nobility that theoretically should have been acquired only by other nobles. However, the distinctions blurred in the face of the financial difficulties of landholders. The town of Bourges received a royal privilege permitting non-nobles to acquire noble land. The fiscal situation in France was also informed by these kinds of distinctions. In the early modern period the famous French royal tax of the *taille* was levied on non-noble lands in the south and on individuals of non-noble status in the north.[1]

Beyond the lands themselves Coeur acquired *rentes* (annuities) and property rights in cash and in kind. Over time the legal concept of land ownership had evolved into a complex matrix of property rights that were divided into rights of use or possession versus abstract rights of ownership. In the course of the Middle Ages, concepts of ownership and possession fragmented further into many rights over land, ranging from simple dues to hospitality rights, to rights to the fruits of the land in sharecropping or usufruct contracts, and later to rental fees and *rentes*. Small monetary payments or dues might be owed the individual who had abstract rights over a particular property, akin to the eminent domain which municipalities can still claim today. Hospitality rights were a carryover from the earlier Middle Ages when lords moved around to take advantage of the produce of particular agricultural estates for the support of their households or the financial resources of a particular town or town inhabitants for their temporary keep during a visit. *Rentes* were a French financial technique of creating a credit line on real property that would produce an annual income. If the annual income or return was not paid, then the creditor could seize the property upon which the *rentes* had been constituted. In the case of agricultural land the crops produced were the source of this income; in regard to urban property, a percentage of the rental sums was designated to pay the annual return. *Rentes* could be for a lifetime or in perpetuity. For example, in the Bourbonnais, Coeur sought to buy up all the *rentes* relating to a specific estate, as a means of ultimately gaining posses-

---

[1] The *taille*, it will be recalled, was a tallage on households and hearths, at times a head tax.

sion of the land itself. In the case of the default of payment of the income due, he could take the property. Coeur was interested in the productivity of the land he meant to acquire, and he attempted to determine this through various means, including the intervention of third parties acting on his behalf. His intention seems to have been to raise the productivity level of these lands, but his fall from grace, his exile, and subsequent death prevented him from realizing significant results. His family obtained possession of some of his holdings in the years after his death, in conjunction with attempts at his rehabilitation.

Coeur also had an interest in urban houses. Over time he acquired or built numerous houses in those towns where his business was concentrated. From an early date he had a house in Saint-Pourçain, the home town of his father, and seven or eight lots and houses in Bourges itself. He ultimately possessed as many as ten properties there. His wife, Macée de Léodepart, had brought to their marriage, in 1418–1420, two of these houses near that of her childhood home in Bourges and a few rural possessions from her father. Their early abode in Bourges, at the corner of the rue des Armuriers and the rue de Linières, was located not too far distant from the site of their future palace. Beyond these holdings coming to Coeur either through inheritance or through his wife's dowry, he acquired warehouse facilities in Bourges as well as elsewhere to accommodate his merchandise.

In other cities, he also had need of space for his trade. Coeur coordinated his interest in urban houses with the territories in which he did personal and royal business. Thus, by 1446 he owned at least three houses, along with other buildings, as many as six in all, in Lyon, and had bought or built houses at Pézenas, Béziers, Beaucaire, and Montpellier in lower Languedoc, and at Marseille in Provence, where he ultimately transferred the management of his Mediterranean affairs in the later 1440s, as noted earlier. In theory, the *Argenterie* followed the king around in his perambulations, but in the mid to late 1440s, Coeur chose to locate the operation in one spot, in Tours, a town of perhaps 12,000 inhabitants in the central Loire River region where Charles VII spent a lot of his time. For this purpose Coeur bought a large house with dependencies in the center of town; at the time of Jean Dauvet's confiscation efforts this structure was judged to be worth about 1200 *écus*.

Here Coeur concentrated the storage facilities and the sales and shipping operations as well as offices, housing for staff, and stables. Beginning in 1445, Coeur began the process of building a mansion in Tours for his own personal use, which might have rivaled his Bourges palace. In Montpellier, he constructed not only a commercial exchange, the *loge*, at great expense to the Montpellier municipality, but also built himself a splendid house. Most of these structures have not survived. However, the palace or great house in Bourges is still standing today.

The palace of Jacques Coeur, as it is commonly termed, is a remarkable example of mid-fifteenth-century domestic architecture. (See photo on p. 10.) The house was constructed on high ground in a quarter of the town of Bourges not too distant from the cathedral. It must have been challenging for Coeur to acquire enough terrain in the already built-up urban center to construct such an ambitious edifice. The shape of the house was an irregular quadrilateral of three stories, with a large interior courtyard surrounded by reception galleries, where Coeur may have displayed some of his wares. (See photo below.) However, as he had warehouses elsewhere in Bourges for this purpose, it is highly unlikely that he used this magnificent structure for commercial storage.

Interior courtyard of Bourges house. (Kathryn L. Reyerson)

The visitor to the Bourges palace today does not see the original building. The Coeur mansion underwent considerable transformation over the centuries as it served as a town hall and courthouse, and it was restored more or less well in the nineteenth and twentieth centuries. A clock in the entrance tower was removed, for example, in the early twentieth century. Having been seized after the arrest of Jacques Coeur, the house was again in the hands of the Coeur family in 1457; it changed hands several times over the centuries. The great finance minister of Louis XIV, Jean-Baptiste Colbert (1619–1683), acquired the house in 1679 for a brief period before selling it to the town of Bourges as a town hall. If some change in the original structure was inevitable, the layout of rooms remains substantially the same as at the time of Coeur, and the sculptural detail was restored according to remaining fragments.

The sculpture of the current front façade displays two life-size figures in blind windows on either side of the central doorway. (See photo on p. 10.) They are facing away from one another today, whereas when the house was constructed, they apparently faced toward each other and would have gazed on a statue of Charles VII set between them. A miniature in a late fifteenth-century book

Kitchen tympanum of Bourges House. (Kathryn L. Reyerson)

of hours, executed for a member of the Coeur family by an atelier of the Berry and now preserved in Munich, depicts a scene with the Coeur palace as background. The façade of the house is shown to have had a statue of the king in a warlike pose as reconqueror of his kingdom. (Rouen had been retaken by 1449 and Normandy by 1450.) The two figures originally flanking the representation of Charles VII have been interpreted as Jacques Coeur and his wife, Macée de Léodepart; alternatively, they may have been servants awaiting the return of their master, a common decorative theme of the time. Such figures appeared as well on the palace of the duke of Berry in Bourges. Whatever the significance of the remaining façade figures on the actual house, their casual pose and their realistic appearance are consistent with the theme of everyday life that seems to pervade the decor and appointments of the house.

It was general practice, according to the rules of heraldry in the fifteenth century, for the exterior of a private house to contain references to the sovereign or overlord and for interior private spaces to be reserved for the coats of arms and symbols of the owners. However, at the Coeur home in Bourges, Charles VII was represented both outside and in, signifying a special allegiance. The recurring refrains of decoration were hearts (*"coeur"* means "heart" in French), **coquilles St. Jacques** (scallop or cockle shells, the symbol of Coeur's patron saint, Saint James, associated with Santiago de Compostella in Galicia), and *fleurs de lys* (lilies, a symbol of the French monarchy), reflecting Coeur's sense of self, allegiance to his family, and loyalty to France and his king. On other parts of the exterior façade, symbols of Coeur and the king are associated together: a lily with two hearts on a bay of the chapel, coquilles and hearts on a tower staircase with a form of Coeur's motto and the letters R. G., which signify "royal guard" (**real guerdon**). Coeur's heraldic device, which he chose upon his ennoblement in 1441, combined coquilles Saint Jacques and hearts. (See photo on p. 9.) Elsewhere, on a tympanum of a lesser postern entry, this shield of Coeur once had figured between two orange trees, at the feet of an angel with a phylactery or frontlet, a band of leaves on its forehead. According to the art historian Christian de Mérindol, this assemblage of elements recurs on a seal of the same era, used by Coeur in 1450 on an acquittal to the tax collector of Normandy. Within the courtyard Mérindol noted the presence of royal emblems as well.

Also in the courtyard are sculptured reliefs of men and women at their daily tasks. On the tympanum above the central entrance to the house from the courtyard women spinners are portrayed. Coeur's association with drapers at an early age and the importance of cloth exports in his Mediterranean trade could represent an acknowledgment of the origins of his wealth and a reflection of his enterprise. Coeur was in many ways a man of the people, in spite of his high office and ennoblement. Nonetheless, in his case, the ambitions of the man are reflected in the architecture and decor of his magnificent Bourges home. All around the walls of his extensively restored chapel in the Bourges house one reads a version of his famous motto: "A vaillans cuer, riens impossible." ("For the valiant of heart, nothing is impossible."). (See photo on p. 9.) The motto can be found elsewhere in the house as well, on banisters, for example.

The palace of Jacques Coeur is replete with decorative detail that was only possible with deliberate attention from its owners. The hardware of doorways often carries the decorative motifs of hearts and shells. Even nails in the palace were forged in the shape of hearts. Such attention to detail in everyday life that Coeur celebrated in his home reflects his personality and perhaps that of his wife, along with his tremendous pride and ego. The decor mirrors his approach to business itself. An eye for detail was valuable in choosing products, in judging quality, and in keeping track of business affairs. Coeur combined these talents with careful attention to the desires of his clientele.

The comfort level of the Bourges house stands out. The stairways throughout the house are not too steep and not too narrow, making access to the upper stories easy. In every room there is a fireplace with a large, copious hearth and chimney, often replete with decoration. The one notable exception is the large hall housing the hired help, who may have numbered between 100 and 300, where portable braziers may have provided a source of warmth. Winters were said to be so cold in the mid-fifteenth century that even the wine froze. Though there remain a number of fifteenth-century buildings in France, including the palaces of justice at Poitiers and Rouen, there is no comparable domestic edifice for the same period, unless it is the castle of Good King René of Anjou, in the Rhône River town of Tarascon, where some of the same innovations in creature comforts are visible, including a liberal distribution of fireplaces.

Entertainment was clearly intended as a purpose of the Bourges palace. Musicians' loges occur at several points in the house, suggesting that Coeur intended to receive his guests graciously, in the lavish manner that the fifteenth-century embraced. Although the king imprisoned Coeur before the house was completed and before he could really inhabit it, he does seem to have entertained there on several occasions, notably to celebrate the elevation of his son Jean to the archbishopric of Bourges in 1450. Coeur's knack for orchestrating events has already been mentioned in regard to the French procession of the 1448 embassy to Rome; he was also a participant in a magnificent 1449 royal entry into Rouen, discussed below. Coeur had a reputation to maintain, but his house suggests that he was a genuinely hospitable person. His character, to the degree that we can know him, must have been open and engaging enough to establish and maintain the extensive network of friendships and contacts that underpinned his career.

There is a well-provided kitchen with a deep well adjacent. Near one public reception room is a sort of pantry with compartments for ice. Scenes of cooking activities are sculpted above the courtyard entrance to the kitchen. There is a fireplace with a pot on the fire, a man pulverizing something in a mortar, a woman with a platter, and a musician with a horn. (See photo on p. 116.) Here and elsewhere in the decor some have chosen to interpret the iconography as revealing of alchemical practices. A sculptural detail of a staircase may represent Coeur and his wife. He is holding a hammer that in alchemical interpretation would represent the union of heaven and earth. Coeur's trip to the Levant is seen by some as one of initiation to alchemy. His service as a moneyer at the Bourges mint is viewed as prime training for an alchemist, and his farm of the relatively unproductive royal mines in the Beaujolais and Lyonnais a source of precious metal for alchemical experiments.

Within the house one finds traditional medieval scenes: three couples eating fruit and a peasant tournament. A small frieze in the treasure room depicts Tristan and Isolde, with King Mark hiding in the trees, famous figures of medieval French romance,

Ship in stained glass in Bourges house. (Kathryn L. Reyerson)

probably a reflection of the literary enthusiasms of Coeur and his milieu. Certainly all these scenes were meant to entertain Coeur's family and entourage, as well as pleasing the man himself.

Among the most striking artistic touches of the Coeur house in Bourges are two depictions of ships in a large reception hall, one in a bas-relief, the other in stained glass. (See photo above.) Originally there may have been as many as six stained glass windows depicting ships in this room, if a 1636 description is to be believed.[2] The stained glass ship bears the arms of Jacques Coeur (hearts and scallop shells), while the bas-relief, a fully-rigged ship with three sails and oarsmen, carries no identifying mark. The bas-relief was apparently discovered in an attic of the house and placed in the galley room in recent times.

Coeur's own business orientation marked the construction around the central courtyard of three second-floor reception gal-

---

[2] Jean Favière, *L'Hôtel de Jacques Coeur à Bourges* (Paris: Picard, 1992), 105.

leries in which the ceilings were built in the form of ships' keels. (See photo below.) Jean Favière, a recent architectural historian of Coeur's house, viewed as legendary, and at the very least unlikely, that Coeur used his own shipwrights, those who constructed the galleys for his trade in the Mediterranean, to build these ceilings. Still, it is difficult to deny that ships provided the design inspiration, whether the construction was by local craftsmen or maritime builders. Of course the **nave** of a medieval cathedral might also evoke a similar design influence; the French term *nef* applies to a church nave as well as to a ship. Extraordinary beams in the ceilings are used throughout the house.

Other motifs run through the house as well. The tympanum above one access to the chapel on the second floor contains a scene of the Annunciation, which was also the theme of the stained glass window in the Coeur chapel of Bourges cathedral. On either side of the hearth in the chapel were his and her stone chairs in alcoves with private chimneys to keep Coeur and his wife, Macée de Léodepart, warm. Decorating the chimney above Jacques' chair are his motto and his coat of arms. (See photo on p. 9.) Jacques' motto also decorates the chimney above Macée's chair, where it is joined by her coat of arms. The keystone of the chapel displays a

Ceiling of gallery in Bourges house.(Kathryn L. Reyerson)

shield that combines the coats of arms of both Coeur and Macée, incorporating half of his device of hearts and shells and half of hers, which was a star on a field of slanting bars. This union in heraldry may echo a close relationship between the spouses. Reflecting the tight-knit connections with his closest collaborators, Coeur included in the ornamentation of the chapel walls the coats of arms of Pierre Jobert, his factor and a merchant of Bourges; of Guillaume de Varye and his father-in-law; of a bourgeois of Bourges, Jacquelin de Culon; of his own father-in-law, Lambert de Léodepart; and of his own son-in-law, Jacquelin Trousseau, the husband of Coeur's daughter Perrette. Of all these, Guillaume de Varye received the position of honor, according to the French art historian Christian de Mérindol. Here is a remarkable visual representation of the inner circle of the Coeur enterprise.

In a large reception room attached by the northern gallery to the chapel, Mérindol noted that the 1636 inspection revealed stained glass windows showing the arms of Coeur and his relations.[3] Present among the decor were Coeur's shield, along with branches of an orange tree, ostrich feathers, hearts, and two mottoes: *"en bouche close nentre mousche"* ("a fly does not enter a closed mouth") and *"dire, faire, taire"* ("say, do, remain silent"). What better sayings for a merchant and royal official, privy to much that was confidential. The orange tree was a symbol, frequently associated with Coeur, that Mérindol interpreted as reflecting his merchant orientation. Certainly, a Mediterranean inspiration was possible, but further references to alchemy could also be symbolized here.

In the great reception hall one also finds striking tribute to the king. Sculptures depict royal symbols above the doorway to the right of the chimney: the winged stag or *cerf volant* with lilies, a symbol of Charles VII, and the winged doe or *biche*, probably the symbol of the queen, Marie d'Anjou, sister of King René. (See photo on p. 123.) There may also have been present at one time a representation of the consecration of Charles VII at Reims, the king only half clothed in preparation for the anointing of his body with holy oil, an integral part of the ceremony. This hall once had stained glass windows that may have depicted the peers of the

---

[3] Mérindol, 164.

Chimney and doorways in Bourges house. (Kathryn L. Reyerson)

realm. Although one of the friezes in the palace supposedly shows Jacques Coeur and Agnès Sorel, Charles VII's mistress, there is no evidence that Coeur and Agnès were more than friends or acquaintances. If it is indeed they who are represented, Coeur and Agnès may have been depicted as the two people closest to the king.

Scallop shells are the dominant theme in Coeur's wife's bedroom, signaling Macée's loyalty to him and their intimacy. Also depicted in her bedroom is another shared coat of arms. A private corridor leading from Macée's bed chamber provided easy access to Coeur's bedroom and elsewhere in the house. At the top of the house is the money or treasure room, the only room in the house without at least two exits. In this room a corbel element shows an emblem shield with hearts and three money bags in place of the usual shells, evocative of the three balls that signaled a pawn broker. If one visits the house today, one finds two heavily carved chests or strong boxes in the room, seemingly of the correct era.

The concern for hygiene was marked. The water closet (a toilet with a hole in stone seating) was plumbed to conduct the waste away from the house, whereas it could have simply gone over the Roman walls of the city fortification into which the back of the house was built. Probably from his experiences in the Near East

Coeur acquired a taste for the sauna. The sauna room displays a system of heating water and pipes to produce steam. In a small retreat nearby is a place to lie down after the experience.

Given the acknowledgment of Macée's presence through the heraldry of the house, it is very likely that she was a partner in its design and decoration. She would also have had responsibility for running the household of the palace and of other homes where she and Coeur had set up housekeeping. Coeur and his wife followed the artistic lead of the local star, the duke of Berry, who preceded them in Bourges and in the Berry, and of the current royal patron, Charles VII. The construction industry in Bourges in the 1440s was the beneficiary of a long tradition begun by the duke of Berry in the previous century. The legacy of his ateliers of artists and builders, as well as the presence in Bourges of the duke's Sainte-Chapelle and the ducal palace near which Jacques Coeur and Macée had lived during their childhoods, undoubtedly influenced the construction of Coeur's house. There was also the palace of Duke John of Berry at Mehun–sur–Yèvre, not too far distant, depicted in the Limbourg book of hours. Though these artistic traditions were strong in Bourges, Coeur and Macée made their own aesthetic choices in the Bourges palace.

They commissioned numerous pieces of sculpture and stained glass to decorate the palace. Their artistic loyalties were quite local; they purchased primarily French productions, not Italian, in spite of Coeur's silk shop in Florence, and not Belgian, in spite of his entrepôt in Bruges. Although Coeur frequented the Italians, copied some of their business techniques, and generally admired the Medici and the Italy of his era, he and Macée did not imitate their style. Their models were local, and in Bourges with the presence of the ducal and royal courts there was ample inspiration.

Coeur's interests did not incite him to collect the art produced in the great centers of the Low Countries or Italy for art's sake; rather he confined himself to the practical needs of decorating his houses and other constructions. His interest in art related to his trade and his buildings as a means of self-promotion. The care that went into the palace decor is remarkable given the extraordinary amount of traveling in which Coeur engaged. His factor Pierre Jobert was one of the Bourges merchants delegated to supervise the house construction. Macée also may have had a central role in its execution as she would have been present more often in Bourges than Coeur.

The symbolism in the decor of the Bourges house, including the details reflecting the emblematic symbols of the era of Charles VII, appears in some of Coeur's other constructions. Close study of the decorative features described in a contract of construction of the *Grande-Loge* of Montpellier, the commercial exchange begun in that Languedocian city in the late 1440s, has revealed a striking similarity to those of Coeur's Bourges house. Christian de Mérindol has discovered a marked shift in decorative intention for the Montpellier *loge* from the first to the second estimate for its construction. The master builder Simon de Beaujeu described these contracts of 1448 in his testimony to Jean Dauvet in 1454.[4] It seems that the second estimate was produced several months after the first and included plans to enlarge and enhance the structure, notably with a large outdoor staircase and new decor for the doorways. The first estimate noted the order for coats of arms, foliage, and personages. The second estimate called for the arms of Jacques Coeur, those of the city of Montpellier, and a series of emblematic elements that evoked King Charles VII. These included a flying stag, roses, and a regnal banner, as well as stags holding royal arms at the main doorway. Other documents furnish further details about the decor of the doors of the Montpellier *loge*, notably a winged stag, a sun, and a rose or rose bush. Also present was a fruit tree with Coeur's coat of arms hanging from it, and at its foot, rose branches.

From the first to the second estimate Mérindol argued that one passed from the point of view of Coeur "the merchant" to that of his incarnation as a statesman (*"homme du roi"*).[5] Accounting for this shift in the use of emblem and symbol was Coeur's enhanced role as a royal ambassador: to the antipope Felix V at Basel in 1447 and 1449, and in 1448 in the splendid French embassy to the pope in Rome. While Mérindol's is a creative interpretation, there is also the more pragmatic explanation that Coeur was able, or thought he would be able, to spend more than originally planned and, as a result, opted, with the second estimate, for a more elaborate decor.

---

[4] Mérindol, 154–5.

[5] Mérindol, 171–2.

As with his palace in Bourges, Coeur would not have time to profit much from this elaborate construction in Montpellier. Though the *loge* was begun in the mid-1440s, not all of the furnishings were in place before Coeur's arrest in 1451. Certainly, in spite of royal subsidies, the expenditures of the town in the construction of the *loge* contributed to the bitterness of Montpelliérains at the time of Coeur's trial, given what they viewed as his betrayal in abandoning Montpellier for Marseille by the late 1440s.

The building campaign of Coeur and his acquisition of numerous estates bear witness to his material success. The Bourges palace and the Montpellier *loge*, in particular, reveal Coeur's aesthetic tastes and his commitment to a symbolism that advertised himself and his king. Though he rose to high society, in many ways Coeur remained close to his bourgeois origins, reflected in the celebration of daily life in the Bourges palace. This was one mark of his genius. He had the common touch and a knack for details, useful in business, but he was also deeply imbued with a desire to flaunt his wealth. He surrounded himself with sumptuous trappings and clothed himself royally. Coeur admired Philip van Artevelde of the family of urban demagogues who ruled fourteenth-century Flanders before the takeover of the dukes of Burgundy. Though of bourgeois origin and thus non-noble at birth, van Artevelde espoused the life of a prince. Perhaps he was a model for the ambitious Coeur. Van Artevelde dined on silver plate to the music of performers and donned lavish attire of brilliant colors—purple, red, and the bluish gray and white associated with fine squirrel pelts (*menu vair*)—much as the count of Flanders or the duke of Burgundy would have done. As for Coeur, he used only silver plate at the Bourges palace. The chronicler Mathieu d'Escouchy stated that "at all times, in his whole hotel, one served only on silver dishes in whatever place it was."[6] A miniature in the *Vigiles de Charles VII* depicts Jacques Coeur on horseback during the triumphal royal entry into Rouen on 15 November 1449.[7] D'Escouchy did not fail to describe the scene: "Afterwards came the count of Dunois, the lord of la Varenne, seneschal of Poitou,

---

[6] D'Escouchy, II: 282; Mollat, 318.

[7] The miniature is from the *Vigiles de Charles VII* by Martial d'Auvergne, Bibliothèque Nationale, ms fr. 5054, f. 182v.

and Jacques Coeur, *argentier* of the king, all three clothed similarly in jackets of violet velvet. . . ."[8] Jacques Coeur seems to have succeeded in impressing Georges Chastellain (1415–1475), the official chronicler of the dukes of Burgundy, Philip the Good and Charles the Bold. Chastellain, though disdainful of burghers, whom he called "villains," while he himself became a knight of the Golden Fleece in 1473, nonetheless admitted the ennobled Coeur to his hall of fame for the nobility, the *Temple de Bocace*.[9]

Coeur's ability to network, to attract loyalty throughout France among individuals in his employ, was rooted in talents that also allowed him to connect with the powerful while retaining the respect of the humble. He possessed an unusually good business mind; one senses that he rarely missed the opportunity to make money. He was a man of enormous energy, constantly in motion. He enjoyed remarkable success, showcased in his magnificent palace in Bourges. Where he excelled was in the superb coordination of his business, financial, commercial, and mining enterprises with his official roles as tax collector, *argentier*, and ambassador. His was, however, a fragile edifice that would crumble in the early 1450s.

---

[8] D'Escouchy, I: 236; Mollat, 281.
[9] Chastellain, 53–9; Mollat, 346.

VII

Fall from Grace
(1451-1455)

Success often brings with it a dark side. Coeur was a man of tremendous skill whose career was spectacular. He attracted envy and may have damaged others along the way, in either real or perceived ways. He appeared to have unlimited wealth, with houses and lands in abundance. The nineteenth-century historian Pierre Clément argued that favorites of the kings of France often became victims of royal justice, once their usefulness had passed. These were talented royal servants or officials, not sycophantic favorites such as Pierre de la Broce during the reign of Philip III (1270–1285). The fact is that there are cases of this sort in the medieval era, beginning with the great royal financier Enguerrand de Marigny, whose fall came just after the reign of Philip IV (1285–1314). The downfall of Jacques Coeur fits this pattern.

There were many reasons for the fall of Coeur. The death of Agnès Sorel, the king's mistress, on 9 February 1449, introduced a change of faction at the royal court. Agnès had patronized the bourgeois party, to which Coeur belonged. Charles VII, "the king of Bourges," was fickle and insecure, and by 1450 with Agnès gone, Coeur's party fell from a position of influence. In its place was a group less favorable to Coeur and more open to the accusations of his enemies, such as Otto Castellani, an Italian immigrant to France, established in business in Toulouse. The king may have resented his talented *argentier* enough to listen to the complaints of his enemies. Charles was, after all, Coeur's largest debtor. Coeur had other powerful debtors, many of noble rank. He had served his purpose now that the French were winning the Hundred Years War. Permanent taxation permitted the funding of a standing army. Charles VII could lay some of the blame for the discontent caused by taxes on Coeur's mishandling of funds and embezzlement, instead of on royal extravagance or military expenditures. Charles decided to act against Coeur, but this was not his finest hour. The king and Coeur had been close collaborators for at least a decade and a half. Coeur had done much to facilitate the recovery of France and French victories in the Hundred Years War. Arrest, condemnation, and punishment were strange ways to show gratitude.

A large number (some 17) of the 22 accusations against Coeur were generated from among men of Languedoc or transplanted Italian immigrants, long installed there. Most of his antagonists were from the mercantile milieu into which he had inserted himself in the south of France.[1] Two families among them, the Castellani and the Teinturier, were ingrained enemies of Coeur. The Castellani were originally from Florence. Otto Castellani, established in Toulouse as royal treasurer, coveted Coeur's position at the *Argenterie* and actually replaced him as *argentier* for a short time after Coeur's condemnation. Castellani's brother Pierre took charge of the *gabelle* tax in Languedoc after Coeur's fall. Castellani was the catalyst of Languedocian complaints; Coeur's relationship with him had soured sometime after 1444. As of 8 November of that year, they were still closely associated when Coeur served as a witness to the marriage contract of Castellani and the daughter of a venerable Montpellier family, the Alamandin.[2] The ceremony must have been the social event of the year. Thereafter, relations between the two degenerated.

The Teinturiers of Montpellier represented another hotbed of hatred for Coeur. Initially, they had assisted Coeur in establishing

---

[1] These included Secondino Bossavini, Janosso Bucelli, Lorenzo Cervelli, and Paul and Louis Dandréa, among those of Italian background, and Pierre Castel, Philibert de Nèves, Jean Nicolas, Aubert Pavez, Mathieu Salomonique, Bernard de Vaulx, and Bertrand Viol of southern France.

[2] Archives Départementales de l'Hérault, II E 95/431, ff. 92–93): Georges Arnaud. I am indebted to Cécile Béghin-Le Gourrierec for this reference.

himself in Montpellier. The father, Isarn, had been involved in Mediterranean trade at the beginning of the fifteenth century, even possessing a ship, which was uncommon for merchants of Montpellier at this time. Son Pierre was a merchant, and son Michel served as the skipper of one of Coeur's galleys, the *Notre–Dame–Saint–Denis*. In 1446, Coeur rebuked Michel Teinturier for having "rescued" a supposedly Christian slave from Alexandria. Coeur sent the slave back to his Muslim master on the *Notre–Dame–Saint–Michel*, skippered by Guillaume Gimart, thereby alienating the Teinturier family of Montpellier and attracting much criticism from contemporaries. Coeur was afraid that the theft of the slave from his Alexandrian master would jeopardize the relations he had so carefully constructed with the sultan of Egypt and the favors accorded French trade, such as a reduction in commercial taxes. Coeur acted for the purposes of diplomacy to maintain his agreement with the sultan of Egypt and to protect western merchants trading in Egypt. Michel Teinturier testified that once the slave was back in Alexandria, he reverted to the Muslim faith of his master. Coeur broke a religious taboo with his action of returning a Christian slave to a Muslim master. There were two religious orders devoted to the rescue of Christians enslaved in Muslim lands, as this was an issue that preoccupied western Christendom in the Middle Ages. Ill will against Coeur echoed through Catalonia and Provence, at Barcelona and at Marseille. Teinturier was humiliated in the course of this affair and would seek revenge.

Michel Teinturier and Otto Castellani were part of the delegation in September 1450 that complained to Charles VII about the irregularities of Coeur's behavior in the south of France. Coeur had required a retainer of 250 *écus* (375 *l. t.*) annually from 1440 to 1445 to intercede for Montpellier with the king. Other payments were also forthcoming for Coeur's successful mediation to limit Montpellier's tax burden: 200 *l.* for a new salt tax (*gabelle*) for Montpellier and 200 *l.* from a tax on *verdet*, a product of copper acetate used to treat grapevines for disease. When these taxes were renewed for ten years in 1450, Coeur pocketed another 400 *écus* (600 *l. t.*). However, because of the diminished economic and demographic state of Montpellier at this time, another tax on the sales of spices, *verdet*, and pitch, and a benefit of one percent of customs taxes on goods arriving at Aigues-Mortes seemed exorbitant to the locals.

The delegation of enemies led by Castellani and Teinturier accused Coeur of taking more than his fair share of the profits from his farm of the celebrated Languedocian fairs of Pézenas and Montagnac. Other men of Languedoc also supported these allegations.[3] Thus, from a situation of business association with the likes of Michel Teinturier, Paul Dandréa, and Janosso Bucelli, a Florentine in Montpellier, Coeur had become the enemy or, more particularly, the target of envy and ill will. Many Languedocians hoped to profit financially from the fall of Coeur, and some did, taking a share of the spoils.

The historian Louise Guiraud at the turn of the twentieth century, in a study titled "The Alleged Role of Jacques Coeur," argued against any positive benefit to Montpellier and Languedoc from Coeur's operations in the south.[4] Guiraud disagreed with the widely held assessment that Coeur, for one brief moment, put Montpellier back on the economic map, only to move his operations to Marseille, leaving the town high and dry. There is no doubt that the heyday of the trade of Montpellier occurred in the late thirteenth and early fourteenth centuries. Mid-fourteenth-century crises of war, plague, and deteriorating commercial conditions in the Mediterranean dealt a terrible blow to the already waning prosperity of the Languedocian center. The Mediterranean trade of late fourteenth-century and early fifteenth-century Montpellier could not compare with that of its medieval heyday. Nonetheless, the modern historian Jacques Heers has argued that Coeur and Charles VII wished for a time to make of Montpellier a royal entrepôt for the luxury trade of the Mediterranean world and, particularly, via the port of Aigues-Mortes and the galleys of France, a site for monopolizing spice imports into France. Yet, even this aim may have stifled rather than stimulated the trade of merchants in Languedoc.

The locals of Montpellier derived benefits from the presence of Coeur and his business, but they had to pay for his support and his influence in royal circles on their behalf through what were, for all intents and purposes, bribes. Coeur engaged them

---

[3] They included Philippe de Nau, Jean de Vaulx, and Jean de Jambes, who was castellan of the port of Aigues-Mortes.

[4] Guiraud *Passim*.

in extensive expenditures in the establishment of the exchange—the *loge*. He also financed the repair, if only temporarily, of the water links between Lattes, Aigues-Mortes, and the sea and at Aigues-Mortes instituted a tax for unloading merchandise. Guiraud emphasized the expense of Coeur's constructions in Montpellier: the exchange, the fountain, even his own house. She also showed that he had been generously paid for arguing the case of Montpellier in royal circles to obtain a reduction in taxes. Guiraud argued persuasively that Coeur used Montpellier for his own purposes, exploited the advantages it could offer, and left it less favorably situated, in all likelihood, than it had been before his arrival, but his intent was not to damage the town. He was merely pursuing his own interests.

The tenor of complaints from Montpellier about Coeur was echoed elsewhere in France. The requirement of being paid for whatever royal privileges he could direct to suitors certainly did not endear him to these parties. There was a pattern to this behavior. The most scandalous episode occurred in 1445 in connection with the marriage of Jeanne of France, natural daughter of the king of France, to the count of Clermont, who was the bastard son of the duke of Bourbon, a **Prince of the Blood**. Representatives of the duke came to Chinon to discuss the details of this union and were received by Coeur, who informed them that they would have to provide 2000 *écus* to sweeten the Christmas festivities of the royal court with dice and pleasure. Coeur, as a commoner, someone far below these personages on the social scale, though ennobled for his service, was vulnerable to attack because of his wealth, power, and arrogance. In this case he gave offense to members of the high nobility, the traditional blood nobility, through methods smacking of extortion. Charles VII was unaware of these demands at the time, but later he and others viewed Coeur's actions as dishonorable and damaging to the king's reputation.

Given this outrageous behavior, Coeur could appear as an anomaly in his own era. The 1445 incident was particularly brazen, tasteless, and tactless. However, whether Coeur behaved worse than other men of power in the Middle Ages remains open to question. Some of the actions occasioning the many charges leveled against Coeur were representative of the business and official culture of the fifteenth century. There is no proof that he was more corrupt, greedier, or more invidious in his actions—only that he was more successful than most, whether in exploitation or positive initiatives. On the basis of the surviving evidence it is difficult, in fact, to determine the accuracy of all allegations against him. There is little doubt that Coeur manipulated to his advantage every official position he occupied. Though his contemporaries may have frowned upon his greed, he was certainly not unique.

Coeur's accuser Otto Castellani was an unsavory type, as it turned out. Castellani ran afoul of Jean Dauvet during the confiscation investigation in 1453-1457. A certain Guillaume Gouffier, seneschal of Saintonge, testified that he was able to persuade Castellani to write on his behalf to Coeur or Guillaume de Varye to obtain 2000 *écus* of domestic merchandise that he needed because he had recently married, but for which he never paid. Dauvet required that Castellani repay this sum on the threat of arrest and confiscation of his horses and personal affects. Castellani was able to borrow the necessary funds. However, several years after Coeur's downfall, in October 1457, Castellani was accused of practicing magic, giving false testimony, and counterfeiting royal seals. For these crimes he was convicted and removed from office as *argentier*, the post he had assumed at Coeur's dismissal, losing all face and position.

If Castellani is an example of the type of individual who turned against Coeur, the actual accusations were also questionable, as was the criminal procedure. Royal officials arrested Coeur in summary fashion based on innuendo in late July 1451. Royal prosecutors took the next two years to assemble what evidence they could for the charges. The decision to place Coeur in custody in a surprise arrest denied him the possibility of flight. Specific complaints against him were constructed from the investigations following his arrest, suggesting the unorthodox nature of the arrest itself. Once in custody, Coeur was questioned repeatedly and denied access to his closest collaborators. Coeur asked specifically to consult with Guillaume de Varye during an interrogation of 26 June 1452, but this request was denied. As noted earlier, Varye had left France after the imprisonment of Coeur and traveled to Valencia and then Florence. He later joined Coeur in Rome in exile. In June 1452, the investigations of royal commissioners resulted in a dossier based on the interrogation of Coeur himself and on testimonies of witnesses from which the commissioners crafted the final accusations.[5] This dossier, containing serious complaints against Coeur, was presented to the king. That Coeur poisoned the king's mistress, Agnès Sorel, in 1449 led the list and was perhaps the most contrived charge of all. Medical evidence did not weigh in with regard to this charge. The king's physician, Robert Poitevin, undermined the presumption of Coeur's guilt when he determined that Agnès died from a fever contracted during childbirth and not from any poison. A noblewoman, Jeanne de Vendôme, and her associate had levied the false accusation for which they were punished with exile from the royal court. That such a rumor could circulate at court and gain some sway over the king speaks to Charles' insecurities and unreliable nature and to the fear and uncertainty these royal qualities engendered in his entourage. Moreover, Agnès had been the advocate for a bourgeois faction that fell from royal favor after her death. Many outside this faction were willing to believe in Coeur's wrongdoing because they envied the man his wealth and power. Beyond what was clearly a trumped up charge, unfortunately for Coeur, there was much raw material from which to craft complaints.

A series of crimes under the broad umbrella of treason (*lèse-majesté*) figured among the most serious allegations. Coeur was accused of counterfeiting the royal seal. A facsimile resembling the secret little seal was found at the home of a close associate of Coeur in Montpellier. Apparently this seal had been employed legitimately in the 1447 royal embassy to Genoa but then had been retained at Montpellier.

Through his broad range of contacts, Coeur was suspected of colluding with foreign heads of state, with Alfonso V of Aragon and Naples, for example. Coeur may have revealed Charles VII's plans to control Genoa to Alfonso, who in the late 1440s was supporting a noble faction hostile to French interests in that city. Coeur was active on Charles' behalf in Genoa, however, and a little indiscretion would not have been terribly serious. On another level, Alfonso supported Coeur's Mediterranean

---

[5] Robert Guillot, *Le procès de Jacques Coeur (1451–1457)* (Bourges: Imprimerie Dusser, 1974), has studied the archival documents associated with the case.

trading ventures, suggesting close ties. Coeur also had lent Alfonso's son funds. After Coeur's arrest, it will be recalled, Alfonso maintained the safe-conducts for the galleys to trade in areas of the western Mediterranean under his authority.

Another area of concern to Charles VII was Coeur's interaction with the dauphin Louis, with whom the king, his father, had difficult relations. In young adulthood the future Louis XI (1461–1483) supported rebellions against the king, such as the *praguerie* (named after the Hussite revolt), which occurred when Charles VII moved to outlaw private armies of princes at the Estates General of 1439. Louis had been convinced in 1440 to join the rebels, including the duke of Bourbon, and hostilities had occurred in the Bourbonnais, the Auvergne, and the Poitou. Charles VII was fearful of Louis' growing strength. The dauphin angered his father by marrying Charlotte of Savoy on 9 March 1451. The historian Paul Murray Kendall suspected a link between the March 1451 marriage and the arrest of Coeur in July of that same year. Men in correspondence with Coeur facilitated the payment of Charlotte's dowry. The exact nature of the contacts between Louis and Coeur escapes the historical record, but Kendall's suspicions may be justified.

There were also tangential connections between Louis and Coeur. Louis was born in Bourges in 1423, raised in western France, and married a first time at Tours in 1436. He thus had ties to Coeur's region of origin. They shared an interest in salt production. Moreover, Louis' province of the Dauphiné was near Savoy and access to Italy as well as to the rising fairs of Geneva that Louis XI would later try to counter by supporting the fairs of Lyon. Coeur had an interest in Lyon. Coeur was active in Geneva when obtaining the resignation of the antipope Felix V in 1449. At one time Coeur's interventions at Genoa on behalf of the king could have coincided with the interests of Louis in the Dauphiné. Coeur may have lent the dauphin money. More concrete connections also existed. Members of the dauphin's court, his chancellor, his chamberlain, and a counselor were in debt to Coeur, according to the records of Jean Dauvet. But then so were many of the members of Charles VII's court. Yet, the fact remains that occasions were not lacking for interaction between Louis and Coeur. In other instances, men associated with Coeur such as Ravand le Danois and a man from the Berry, Jean Bochetel, seem to have served the dauphin.

Further, the art historian Christian de Mérindol made the compelling claim that the association of Coeur and the dauphin could be discerned in the cathedral of Bourges where the shield of Louis XI occurs repeatedly. To bolster this line of reasoning Mérindol noted that Louis XI, once king, reappointed close associates of Coeur who had suffered as a result of the latter's disgrace. It is remarkable that Louis XI favored some of Coeur's closest collaborators after Coeur's death and when he, Louis, had become king. Guillaume de Varye regained royal favor under Louis XI, who appointed him to the *Argenterie* again in 1461. At the time of Coeur's arrest, Guillaume's brother, Simon de Varye, was imprisoned, only to be liberated and reinstated as a clerk of the *Argenterie*. Simon was still associated with the *Argenterie* as late as 1457, when he was in charge of the stables. The reinstatement of Coeur's associates goes considerable distance toward validating the claim that Coeur was falsely accused. These arguments suggest that Louis XI had a close tie to Bourges and that he retained respect for the skill of Coeur's associates. But even with a connection between the men, there is no evidence that Coeur supported Louis over Charles; Louis XI did nothing to assist Coeur after his arrest.

Coeur's relations with another head of state, King René of Anjou, also caused concern. Here too geographic considerations bearing on economic operations may have dictated Coeur's involvement. René had Mediterranean connections, and he ruled Provence, in which lay the desirable port city of Marseille. Provence, as part of René's Angevin kingdom, was not subject to the intervention of the French king. It was a source of salt and coral for trade in the Mediterranean world. The southern end of the great Rhône River corridor, which facilitated transport in eastern France, also lay within Provence.

One might even add the papacy to the list of foreign powers with whom Coeur had interacted, sometimes for his own benefit, but often on behalf of the king of France, for example, in regard to the negotiation of the withdrawal of the antipope Felix V and in the context of the 1448 embassy to Rome. In all these areas, proof of treason was difficult to assemble. However, the presumption of treason certainly colored the nature of the proceedings against Coeur and tipped the balance of sentiment against him.

Beyond the interactions with foreign powers, accusations of treason included trading in arms to the enemy, notably the Muslims. The 1440s and early 1450s were a period when eastern Christendom was severely threatened. The sultan of Egypt had designs on the island of Rhodes, a possession of the Hospitallers, and an important trading station for westerners in the Near East. Coeur negotiated a treaty between the Knights of Rhodes and the sultan in 1445. The Ottoman Turks had made inroads in the Near East and conquered Constantinople in 1453. The stakes were high in any traffic in arms between Christian and Muslim, which was theoretically prohibited by the papacy and western monarchs. Coeur himself benefited from papal dispensation for his cross-cultural trade with Muslims, it will be recalled. In regard to the accusation of arms trading, Coeur argued that he had only sent arms to Egypt as symbolic or testimonial gifts to the sultan from the king of France and that there was no real arms trade, but witness testimonies in the information-gathering phase of the lawsuit suggest a more sustained operation. One witness, the royal furrier André Jobert, stated that he had seen a Venetian galley at Alexandria bring in casks full of arms from the region of Milan, a center of weapons manufacture in Italy.[6] According to Jobert, Jean de Village, who was in Alexandria with Coeur's galleys, seized the owner of the casks and would have done him harm had he not feared a controversy with the Venetians. The witness gave a treasonous spin to Village's behavior in this incident, suggesting the source of Village's negative reaction was antagonism to competition, but the opposite interpretation is just as likely. Village could have been attempting to thwart the traffic in arms to the infidel. Coeur's enemy Michel Teinturier, who had been humiliated in the slave incident discussed above, testified shortly thereafter that swords and daggers were transported on a galley of Coeur's under Guillaume Gimart as skipper. Certainly, traffic in arms was strictly and officially forbidden, and it reflected poorly on the honor of the king of France if his merchants were so engaged.

Finally, two further incidents of treason dishonored the king. Coeur ordered silver plate, jewelry, and low-grade metal coins melted down at the mints of Avignon, Montpellier, and Rhodes. Then he had ingots of poor quality stamped with the mark of the

---

[6] Guillot, 36.

king of France, the *fleur de lys*, and exported to the Levant. The offense was two-fold. First, the low precious metal content of the ingots, the quality of which was not lost on the Muslims, was an insult to the king's reputation, and, second, the trade itself—export of precious metal to the infidel—was forbidden. Technically speaking, Coeur was probably raising funds to support the king's war effort, but once the king withdrew his favor, it was possible to construe such actions differently. The second incident was the episode of Coeur's extortion with regard to the marriage of Jeanne of France to the count of Clermont, noted above. Coeur's actions were said to have impugned the honor of the king.

Prosecutors also used the old accusation of coinage falsification against Coeur, recalling the 1427 charge of coining money of inadequate precious metal purity and weight against Coeur, Ravand le Danois, and their associates at the Bourges mint, though later remitted by the king in 1429, and the other coinage offense of 1430. In spite of the renewal of accusation against Coeur, Ravand le Danois continued in his office of master of the mint until 1461. Although these were very serious issues, the misdeeds already had been forgiven, as men with the technical expertise of minter were much in demand in the kingdom of Charles VII. In this lawsuit, however, royal lawyers would stop at nothing to indict Coeur.

Coeur's involvement in law of marque proceedings in the 1440s was the subject of considerable controversy causing him difficulties after his arrest. In the decree of condemnation of 29 May 1453, issued by King Charles VII of France, among the many charges leveled against his *argentier* was the following: "And in addition the said Coeur was found charged by the said information to have exacted and unduly obtained several large sums of *deniers* from the marques of the Genoese, of Provence and of Catalonia. . . . "[7] The last interrogations of Coeur under torture produced information about manipulation of funds in regard to marques, but perhaps for a good cause, the war. This and the pressure of months of imprisonment and interrogation led to his admission of guilt on most of the points of the accusations against him.[8] The case against Coeur was grim indeed.

---

[7] Guillot, 108–14, published the entire decree.

[8] Guillot, 84–107, published the transcript of the last interrogations of Coeur.

Macée did what she could to preserve their belongings after the arrest of her husband, though the situation must have been very difficult for her. She retreated to a rural estate for part of the time, it would seem. A woman alone in the Middle Ages was always at risk. After Coeur's arrest, Macée may have been sustained by the presence of her son Jean, the archbishop of Bourges. But her every action was undoubtedly subject to suspicion. She was criticized on one occasion for having lent tapestries to Jean for a church-related reception he was organizing. Later, Jean Dauvet and the king's officials would level the accusation, for which there is some basis, that trappings were removed from the Bourges house to prevent their confiscation and sale by the king's men. In fact, Macée spirited away most of the linen, silver dishes, and other furnishings from the Bourges palace to a rural property, Menetou-Salon, as early as November 1451, several months after Coeur's arrest. These goods may well have been associated with her dowry and thus theoretically immune from confiscation by Dauvet. Later, Coeur's children would make this argument in order to recover property that had been seized.[9] That Macée remained devoted to her husband until her death in 1452 is without doubt. On Coeur's side, his loyalty and affection seem to have been equally strong. Visually and materially, the Coeur house in Bourges (described in detail in Chapter 6) reflects the integral part that Macée played in her husband's life.

Salvage actions, similar to those of Macée in Bourges, were carried out by Perrette, Coeur's niece, the wife of Jean de Village, in the south of France. She did what she could for Coeur after his arrest, with the help of factors, associates, and friends, facilitating the removal of clothing, gold objects, cloths, and tapestries from Coeur's house in Montpellier, so that these valuable items would not fall into the hands of Jean Dauvet. A certain Jean de Beaune, clerk of the *Argenterie*, who was established in Montpellier, admitted under interrogation that Perrette had requested his aid in transporting goods to Marseille for the contrived purpose of a pilgrimage.[10] Other documents and merchandise were spirited out of France through Avignon and Aigues-Mortes.[11]

---

[9] Guillot, 73–4.

[10] Mollat, 111–112.

[11] Guillot, 69.

If Coeur's relationships began in Bourges with his family and their commercial contacts, they extended out in ever widening circles as he became more powerful within fifteenth-century France. He had the gift of attracting people to him at all levels of the social hierarchy, in both secular and ecclesiastical society. The efforts of the clergy to assist Coeur after his arrest are noteworthy in this regard. Jacques Juvénal des Ursins, bishop of Poitiers, where Coeur had been transferred in or before the spring of 1453, sent his vicars to Lusignan on 26 May 1453 to convince the king that Coeur, who was a widower since the death of Macée de Léodepart at the end of 1452, should be turned over to ecclesiastical justice as a lapsed churchman.[12] The attachment of Coeur as a youth to the ducal chapel in Bourges was the basis of this claim. If his entry into holy orders, even lower orders, had been recognized, he might have benefited from a more lenient form of justice before an ecclesiastical, rather than a royal or secular court. The motives for Jacques Juvénal des Ursins' intervention are unknown. Jacques Juvénal appears to have been a friend of Coeur. However, his actions could have stemmed from politics or internal family rivalries. In supporting Coeur, he took a position contrary to that of his illustrious brother, the chancellor of France, Guillaume Juvénal des Ursins, who was closely associated with the king and sided with Charles VII against Coeur. Other factors also complicated the request that Coeur be considered a clergyman. The judicial officer of the diocese of Poitiers, Jean Tripault, was the brother of Guillot Tripault, a servant of Coeur who managed the Bourges palace, and was thus closely associated with the accused. These connections made the bishop of Poitiers' attempts futile. The request could be viewed as special pleading on behalf of Coeur's supporters, with its substance perhaps contrived to get Coeur off with a light punishment. Whatever the motivation, Jacques Juvénal des Ursins' efforts were unsuccessful.

Coeur's links with the clergy were multiple and were encouraged by family ties. As noted earlier, his brother Nicolas became bishop of Luçon after having been a canon of the cathedral at Bourges, a position Coeur's oldest son, Jean, would also hold in his rise to the archbishopric of Bourges. His half brother Jean

---

[12] Guillot, 54–6.

Baquelier was also a canon there. Coeur's son Henri was a dean and canon at Limoges. Coeur had been instrumental in the promotion of his sons in the Church and also assisted children of his colleagues, acquaintances, and clients in their ecclesiastical ambitions. He did favors for churchmen, transmitted messages, and offered them prized items from the *Argenterie* stores, such as camel skins for the king's confessor, Gérard Machet, who in turn assisted Coeur's sons, Jean and Henri, in their careers.

From all evidence, Coeur himself had at least a conventional faith. He was a major benefactor of the Bourges cathedral in the later 1440s, went on personal pilgrimage at Montserrat in Catalonia in 1445, and died on a papal crusade to Rhodes in 1456. Just as the early Capetian Hugh Capet's good relations with the clergy aided him in gaining the French throne in 987, so Coeur's religious connections were of great assistance to him throughout his life.

The relations between Coeur and the confessor of King Charles VII were close. Gérard Machet, a moderate **Gallican** like Coeur, and thus a supporter of a French Church independent of Roman control, called Coeur "my true friend" (*"verus amicus meus"*).[13] There must have been a real bond between the two men to elicit such terms of endearment on the part of Machet, something for which Machet's correspondence provides evidence. Machet was also closely tied to Coeur's brother, Nicolas, and to others of their entourage. If Machet had been alive in 1451, the accusations against Coeur might have found less favor with the king.

With the loss of significant allies, Agnès Sorel and Gérard Machet, Coeur could not have been ignorant of the threats posed by his enemies. He must have been aware of the resentment caused by his ascension to power as someone who could be considered an upstart in society, thus turning traditional society on its head. He should have been aware of the uneasiness that such a rise above one's station would cause. The chronicler Mathieu d'Escouchy emphasized the jealousy of other merchants since, according to d'Escouchy, Coeur earned more than all the other merchants in the kingdom combined and was the envy of the great lords of the kingdom, who turned against him.[14] However, power and wealth could

---

[13] Mollat, 297.

[14] D'Escouchy, II: 282–2; Clément, I: XII–XIV.

be inebriating, and Coeur could also have believed that he enjoyed the genuine friendship of the great, as indeed he did in the case of Pope Nicholas V, King René of Anjou, and Alfonso V. He may have believed that Charles VII felt genuine friendship, loyalty, and gratitude toward him, enough to resist the negative propaganda circulated by Coeur's enemies. "I am as well viewed by the king as I ever was," he wrote to his wife in July 1451.[15] Jacques' assurances to Macée that he still had the good will of the king may have simply been his attempt to reassure her and spare her from worry. He himself must have been aware of the change in the wind, but a man enjoying his level of power and influence may have had difficulty coping with reality. Alas, Charles VII would not prove loyal, and Coeur was arrested before the end of July 1451.

Regarding all of the accusations leveled against him, Coeur initially denied wrongdoing. He was gradually worn down by interrogation and torture. After his wife's death in late 1452, the extraordinary, even unorthodox, court process relating to his case extracted a concession under torture from him: "I will admit to anything you wish."[16] On 29 May 1453, Charles VII issued the sentence condemning Coeur for high treason.[17] However, thanks to the intercession of Pope Nicholas V, the death penalty was commuted to permanent banishment along with the confiscation of Coeur's goods until 100,000 *écus* of debts to the royal treasury and 300,000 *écus* of fines were paid to the king. Coeur was to remain incarcerated until he paid these sums; thereafter he was to be banished from the kingdom. He was also required to perform a ceremony of honorable amends (*amende honorable*), a public penance common in the Middle Ages. Before the ceremony of amends, Jacques Juvénal des Ursins again contacted his brother the chancellor via vicars who brought with them the letters of tonsure for Coeur (head shaving was characteristic of men in church office) in another effort to get him declared a churchman and thus no longer adjudicable by royal justice. But once again the response was negative, and the request was not

---

[15] Mollat, 284.

[16] Guillot, 46.

[17] See note 5 above.

granted a hearing.[18] Thereupon, Coeur made amends before the royal council, dressed only in a shirt and on his knees, carrying a heavy wax candle.

The fifteenth-century "press" was non-existent, but chronicles of the time filled some of the same role in commenting on Jacques Coeur, his career, and his fall. The chronicler Mathieu d'Escouchy recounted the downfall of Coeur in some detail.[19] He placed emphasis on the modest origins of the man and on his talents of good sense, valiant spirit, and good behavior. He attributed the conquest of Normandy to Coeur's encouragement of the king and to his tremendous financial support. After having narrated briefly the achievements of Coeur in his own right and on behalf of his male children, d'Escouchy stated that fortune turned away from him. Word spread that it was not possible for a man of such humble beginnings to do all he did, to have traded in such merchandise and invested in landed estates, to have served only on silver dishes in his house, without having used the king's money to pay for this display. D'Escouchy then rehearsed the litany of charges against Coeur, the episode of the Christian slave and the poisoning of Agnès Sorel among them.

Coeur, according to d'Escouchy, denied that he had taken the king's money, but rather, due to the king's generosity, he had succeeded in trade in which he had, as the chronicler stated, earned his "*vaillant.*"[20] Coeur also denied a role in the affair of the Christian slave, distancing himself by stating that his galleys traveling in Muslim lands returned to him once in two years. He further denied poisoning Agnès, for which he would ultimately not be condemned. He recounted how, after agreeing to loan the king money for the Normandy campaign, in the amount of 200,000 *écus*, he had asked if he could send the sultan of Egypt a harness from the king, which he did through Jean de Village, to the great pleasure of the sultan.[21] In Coeur's view the arms trade of which he was accused was really the result of diplomatic gifts.

---

[18] Guillot, 56.

[19] D'Escouchy, II: 280-9. See also my discussion in the forthcoming article, "Le procès de Jacques Coeur," *Les procès politiques (XIVe–XVIIe siècle)* (Rome: Ecole française de Rome, forthcoming).

[20] D'Escouchy, II: 285; Clément, I: XVII.

[21] On the amount of Coeur's loans to the king, see also Chastellain, *Oeuvres*, VII: 92.

In his *Mémoires*, Jacques Du Clercq (1420–1501), a Flemish lawyer and chronicler of the Burgundian duke, cited Coeur's humble origins in conjunction with his description of the triumphal entry of Coeur, the seneschal of the Poitou, and the count of Dunois into Rouen after the Normandy conquest. Du Clercq noted the motto of Coeur and the lavish house in Bourges. Du Clercq mentioned Coeur's imprisonment, with a brief reference to the escape to Rome where Coeur lived as honorably as in France from merchandise, presumably in trade, which he had outside the kingdom. He estimated Coeur's fortune, taken by the king, at one million in gold *écus*.[22]

This sum was undoubtedly a gross exaggeration, indicative only of the order of magnitude of Coeur's wealth in the contemporary imagination. In his efforts to confiscate Coeur's wealth Jean Dauvet found no evidence of a fortune this large. However, in evaluating Coeur's reputation for riches, it is useful to consider the levels of wealth in the late Middle Ages. The merchant Salimbene Salimbeni of Siena, a member of the Salimbeni company, could make his city a gift of 118,999 *l*. Sienese in 1260, when Siena was at war with Florence.[23] The city of Montpellier itself was sold to King Philip VI of France for 133,000 florins in 1349, and Pope Clement VI bought Avignon from the queen of Naples for 80,000 florins in 1348.[24] In 1318 the Bardi company of Florence closed their books at 870,000 florins.[25] In 1451 the Medici of Florence had assets of about 75,000 florins.[26] When Coeur was condemned in 1453, it will be recalled that he was required to pay a total of 400,000 *écus* in debts and fines to the king. For the ransom of King John the Good after his capture at the battle of Poitiers in 1356, all of France managed to raise only 450,000 florins.[27] Coeur said he could not pay the

---

[22] Du Clercq, 618; Clément, I: XX.

[23] The Sienese lira was worth slightly less than the Florentine florin.

[24] The comparable sums in *écus* and *livres tournois* for Montpellier were 120,000 *écus* or about 150,000 *l. t.* with the *écu* worth 25 *s. t.* at that time and for Avignon about 72,250 *écus* or about 90,000 *l. t.*

[25] About 700,000 *l. t.* at that time.

[26] 88,750 *l. t.*

[27] At the conversion rate of the florin at 5/6 of an *écu*, this was only a slightly smaller sum.

400,000 *écus*, although his fortune has been calculated as greater than that amount, but perhaps not the alleged million.

Another contemporary to comment on Coeur's fall was Thomas Basin. Basin, bishop of Lisieux in Normandy, had a stormy career, first favored by Charles VII and then in disfavor and exile at Louvain under Louis XI for his support of the king's brother, the duke of Normandy. Basin sang of Coeur in memorable prose, calling him "the most industrious and ingenious of men."[28] Among the accusations against Coeur, Basin mentioned the provision of arms and other illicit merchandise to the Muslins and the illegal appropriation of sums from his administration of Languedoc.

Georges Chastellain, chronicler of the Burgundian dukes, took note of Coeur in his *Temple de Bocace*, remarking on the envy in which Coeur's great fortune was held.[29] It was Chastellain who spoke of Coeur in oft-repeated terms as a man of great industry, skill, and guile. Chastellain recalled Coeur's role in bringing profit and glory to Charles VII. Then Fortune, which had brought him to the summit, reversed itself. The medieval period used the topos of Fortune as a wheel, with the image of "what goes up must come down."

The many accusations, noted above, and the ill will of the envious together brought down a valiant man. Charles VII's rejection of his loyal *argentier* must have been a heavy blow to Coeur. Yet, this was not the end of him. His beloved wife was dead. His children were adults and well placed. Coeur could now plan his escape from prison and leave France for good. Though he never gave any indication of having lost his commitment to France and its king, to remain in his native land would have meant perpetual imprisonment. His recuperative powers were great, and his ambition and optimism clearly undiminished. Moreover, as later statements by Pope Nicholas V suggest, Coeur harbored hopes that he could vindicate himself before the king of France. Perhaps he aimed at another pardon. (See Chapter 8.)

In the last days of October 1454, word came to the king of France that Coeur had escaped from his prison in the castle of Poitiers after 39 months of confinement and torture, 16 follow-

---

[28] Basin, II: 151–3; Clément, I: XXIII–XXVI.

[29] Chastellain, *Bocace*; 53–9; Clément, I: XXI–XXII.

ing his official condemnation by the royal court of King Charles VII (29 May 1453). Jean Dauvet, the royal legal representative and, for the modern historian, invaluable record keeper, who had been ordered by the king to proceed with the confiscation of Coeur's property after his condemnation, learned the news of his escape from Poitiers upon arriving in Lyon on 29 October.[30] Charles VII ordered Dauvet to search all ports and roadways to locate the escaped prisoner. The latter wrote messages and sent messengers to Languedoc, west of the Rhône in southern France, to Provence in what is today southeastern France, to Mâcon and Chalon in the eastern French province of Burgundy, and elsewhere, and to the ports and roadways of the Lyonnais, south of Burgundy. Just a few days later, on All Saints Day (1 November 1454), Coeur was discovered in religious **asylum** in the church of Dunet near Montmorillon in central France. The king sent a counselor of the French high court, the *Parlement de Paris*, to negotiate with Coeur for his surrender. Word reaching the king's household that Coeur had been retaken was jubilantly received but erroneous. Instead of giving himself up, Coeur was on the move again, evading his trackers to gain asylum at Limoges in the monastery of the **Jacobins**, a **Dominican** house beyond the reach of the king. (See map on p. 13.)

In the Middle Ages asylum could take many forms. For serfs fleeing their masters, towns offered refuge. The medieval law of religious asylum dictated that someone pursued by a public authority might request asylum in a church or monastery and remain there in safety from arrest by public officials, though there was generally a time limit, 40 days, during which asylum was valid. Churches and monasteries assumed an important role within the criminal justice system as a result. In France in 1205 at the accords of Paris and again at the royal assembly of Vincennes in 1329, royal jurisdiction gained some control over fugitives, above and beyond ecclesiastical prerogatives, but it was by no means complete. In the mid-fifteenth century, the protection of asylum was still such that royal officials did not violate the sanctuary of Coeur's refuge. Asylum was one ploy in his great escape from France.

---

[30] The best treatment of Coeur's escape is that of Antoine Thomas, "L'Evasion et la mort de Jaques Cuer," *Revue Historique* 98 (1908): 72–86.

The monks and friars of the houses where he sought asylum were courageous in receiving him, as they were assuming risks. The king's men could always take measures into their own hands. Dunet was a dependency of the great abbey of Saint-Martial de Limoges. There may have been behind-the-scenes connections between monks at Dunet and Limoges to assist Coeur on his way as part of a well-articulated plan of escape. The Jacobin house at Limoges lay outside the city fortifications on a large hillside overlooking the Vienne River and the Saint-Martial bridge. It represented a good place to take refuge and to benefit from asylum. Though Limoges was a bit of a detour, plotting of his escape route on the map of France makes it clear that Coeur was headed for southeastern France in order to cross the Rhône River into Provence. (See map on p. 13.) Once in Angevin Provence, Coeur would be free of French justice.

The stayover at Limoges may have had several purposes. Coeur had local contacts there, and his escape furnishes examples of the loyalty of his business associates. Besides family support from his son, Henri, a canon of the cathedral of Limoges, Coeur did business with Jean Quercin, merchant and guardian of the royal seal in the *bailliage* (administrative district) of Limoges, and Quercin was instrumental in helping him during his escape to freedom outside France. At Limoges, Quercin, it will be recalled, was a liaison in Coeur's commercial network between the Mediterranean world and the *Argenterie*. Quercin visited Coeur in the Jacobin monastery and may have given him money. Coeur was able to leave Limoges without capture. Because of his association with Coeur, Quercin and several of his relatives were arrested by officials of the king of France and interviewed several times about Coeur's escape. The judicial process dragged on until 1456–1457, when Quercin finally received an order from the *Parlement de Paris* relieving him of further legal difficulties stemming from his role in the escape of Jacques Coeur.[31] Aid to Coeur had cost him more than two years of legal harassment. Here is someone who could have denounced Coeur and perhaps disengaged himself from his financial obligations to him. That he remained loyal and assisted Coeur's escape is testimony to the high regard in which the latter was held by his associates.

---

[31] Thomas, 79–80.

Coeur's destination was the royal administrative site of Beaucaire in Languedoc on the Rhône River, facing Tarascon and the lovely fifteenth-century castle of King René in Angevin Provence. Across the river was freedom. Along the route from Limoges to Beaucaire, Coeur likely sought out refuge in religious houses benefiting from asylum. Dauvet stated in his journal that he received letters on 11 February 1455 from the king at Lyon announcing that Coeur had left Limoges and that Dauvet once again should make certain that all ports and roadways were guarded. The king's men were right on the heels of Coeur. Dauvet wrote letters to the provost of Mons and elsewhere in Languedoc ordering that all be diligent. Shortly afterward, Dauvet reported he had word that Coeur was in Beaucaire. Thus, by about 12 February 1455, Coeur had reached the French frontier on the Rhône River.

At Beaucaire, Coeur hid with the **Cordeliers** in their Franciscan house. The king's men quickly located him and, upon the refusal of the friars to surrender their refugee, surrounded the Cordelier house with guards. There were houses of both Cordeliers and Jacobins in late medieval Bourges. Coeur may have been familiar with them and connected to some of their occupants. At any rate, he seems to have been able to gain assistance through asylum from a network of churches and monasteries along his route.

The friars' houses offered protection for the escaped prisoner, and royal officials chose to respect their privilege of asylum, but other dangers lurked for Coeur in Beaucaire. There was an attempt on his life, organized by one of his most ardent enemies, Otto Castellani. In one version of this aggression, Coeur managed to beat off his assailant with a lead mallet. At about the same time, an attempt was made to poison Coeur with arsenic powder in his wine. Coeur apparently drank some of this and lay close to death for six days. These details have survived in a letter written by Coeur to Jean de Village in Marseille.

About February 1455, from his hideout in Beaucaire, Coeur, in fact, made a desperate appeal to Jean, very likely through this letter, to come to his aid before it was too late. That Coeur got a message to Jean de Village for assistance is confirmed by a later royal letter of pardon regarding Jean's participation in the subsequent events. Coeur's letter was extant in the mid-nineteenth century when Pierre Clément judged it authentic and published the version surviving today.[32] Arguing for its authenticity are several elements, among them, the initials of J. C. as in Jacques Coeur, J. D. V. as in Jean de Village, and G. D. V., as in Guillaume de Varye, these two being the closest collaborators of Coeur.

The letter began, "Jean, my good nephew, dear son, for as much as you are bound to me by the affinity of love and my life is dear to you, do not delay in coming to take me out of this franchise, given that within five days they will seize me from it and put me to death or kill me within, which would already have happened without this good brother Hugault. . . ." Coeur told Jean that he had attracted the sympathy of a Cordelier brother, Hugault; this friar was possibly the messenger who made contact with Jean at Marseille. In his letter Coeur implied that Hugault had supplied him with sufficient money for necessities and made him wear jewels hidden in a belt around his waist. He urged Jean to trust the brother completely. At the end of the letter Coeur invoked the close ties linking him with Jean. "And for God, dear son, do not let me succumb for all that you are dear." Coeur feared for his life.

Jean de Village wasted no time, journeying to Tarascon in Provence, just across the Rhône River from Beaucaire, outside the territory of the king of France, and communicating with Coeur via the Cordelier brothers of Tarascon. Village then returned to Marseille and rounded up two ship captains, Guillaume Gimart and Gaillardet de Boursa, formerly in the employ of Coeur's galleys. In an armed boat, these captains, with a crew of perhaps 20, sailed up the Rhône River to Beaucaire at night. This group surreptitiously entered the city through a breach in the walls and secured access to the Cordelier house with assistance from brothers loyal to Coeur. They then rescued Coeur and took him to Tarascon. What happened during the rescue is unclear. In testimony after the event, Jean de Village insisted there was no bloodshed. His firm loyalty to Coeur, as well as that of Gimart, Boursa, and the others, is patent in this daring rescue mission. However, other evidence suggests that there had been a violent struggle in which those who would have done harm to Coeur were wounded, even mortally.

---

[32] Mollat, Annexes 3. XII: 391–2, had doubts about the authenticity of the letter, which he nonetheless reproduced. The original of the letter has disappeared.

Brother Hugault, the Cordelier friar, took huge risks for Coeur, and he paid for this service since he was listed along with Coeur's associates, accused of aiding and abetting the prisoner, in the judicial inquests regarding the Beaucaire escape. An inquest held at Arles in Provence cited Jean de Village, Guillaume Gimart, Gaillardet de Boursa, Jean Forest, and the Cordelier in question "as servants and those close to Jacques Coeur."[33] All of these individuals received royal letters of pardon for their actions in assisting Coeur after they had entered a request with the royal judicial machinery.[34]

Once in Tarascon, Jacques Coeur was outside France, and he was again a free man, benefiting from the good graces of King René. From Tarascon Coeur made his way to Rome through towns such as Port-de-Bouc, Marseille, Nice, Pisa, and Florence, shepherded by Jean de Village. Officers of the French king attempted to get him extradited from Provence, Pisa, and Florence, but their efforts were either too late or to no avail. On 14 June 1455, the Council of Florence responded to an inquiry by the king of France that if Coeur had passed through Florence, it had not come to their attention. While Coeur was well known in the city and had established a silk shop there, in his escape he undoubtedly kept a low profile. Then too, he may have enjoyed the support and assistance of the Italian business community in these Tuscan towns.

Coeur's escape from France reveals a network of religious connections and personal relations upon which he could rely. Most of his associates remained faithful to him in the face of great pressure by the monarchy and of considerable danger to themselves personally and to their families. For his own family to remain loyal was perhaps to be expected, but the ties Coeur had developed with his business associates held firm as well. Men like Jean Quercin did not betray him, even though they might have profited from his capture and fall from the king's grace. The assistance Coeur received is a tribute to the high regard in which he was held by those around him. His children and their families must have been

---

[33] Mollat, 292–3.

[34] The letter of remission for Jean de Village came in February 1457 (n.s.). See Thomas, 80.

thrilled at the escape of their father, though their involvement is more difficult to trace in the particulars. Henri's placement in Limoges and Nicolas' connections in Rome were undoubtedly influential in Coeur's successful escape and exile.

King René of Anjou served as Coeur's protector at the time of his arrest, condemnation, and escape, permitting him to pass through Provence in order to reach Rome. Earlier, René had stymied the efforts of Jean Dauvet to extradite Jean de Village from Marseille in order to investigate Coeur's business and, especially, to confiscate Coeur's wealth. After the arrest of the *argentier* in 1451, King René allowed the four galleys of Jacques Coeur, active in the Mediterranean, to seek safe harbor in Marseille and to continue to sail on behalf of his affairs, managed by Jean de Village. Coeur's goods and possessions had been shipped from Montpellier to Provence and found refuge in the lands of King René. Certainly after the fact, if not before, Coeur's involvement with King René could have given pause to the king of France. King René had to navigate difficult diplomatic waters, not wishing to alienate his brother-in-law, the king of France, but determined to protect Jacques Coeur.

In the end the personal ties Coeur forged saved his life by permitting his escape. His contacts ran the gamut, from highly placed individuals in secular and ecclesiastical society, to his business associates and to monks and friars scattered in religious houses across France. The remaining evidence confirms that however demanding he was, however ambitious and even greedy, Coeur had charisma. He was a man open to others, given to friendships, and clearly someone who inspired loyalty in the face of great danger and much pressure from the royal power structure. When Coeur escaped across the Rhône, he would never again see France. The last chapter in Coeur's life opens in Rome where he made a new beginning.

VIII

Exile, Crusade, and Death (1455–1456)

Coeur spent the years from 1455 to his death in 1456 outside France. These were surely years filled with sadness and loneliness over the loss of Macée and the separation from his family and homes and the culture he knew best. However, exile in Rome allowed Coeur a new life of privilege at the papal court. He reestablished himself financially through trade, and he made himself useful to the pope in a fashion that resembled his official role in France. His participation on the papal crusade to Rhodes against the Turks in 1456 would mark the last act of his career as he lost his life at Chios from wounds of battle.

When Coeur arrived in Rome at the end of his escape route, he sought out Pope Nicholas V, whom he knew well from past diplomatic contacts. Pope Nicholas, though near death at Coeur's arrival, addressed the cardinals on Coeur's behalf on 16 March 1455, speaking of the many favors that he had performed for the papacy, arguing for his innocence of all accusations, and urging that Coeur be supported in his efforts to prove himself to the king of France.[1] There is no evidence that Coeur was embittered as a result of his betrayal by Charles VII. In the same address, the pope stated that Coeur had received as much as 100,000 ducats from

---

[1] Kerr, 264–5, has published a translation of this decree in the Consistory. He also included a photograph of the original document. Nicholas said, "And we charge you to favor and justify his cause before the King and all other persons whatsoever. . . ."

the pope and procured many things for him, for which he had been persecuted.[2] Nicholas V had intervened earlier with the king of France on Coeur's behalf after his arrest in 1451 and in order to get the death sentence of 1453 commuted to banishment. After Coeur's death, in the proceedings undertaken by his son, Jean Coeur, to gain the rehabilitation of his father's good name, the testimony of Guillaume d'Estouteville, archbishop of Rouen and cardinal of Ostia, recalled the relations between Nicholas V and Coeur; d'Estouteville stated that the pope had been very fond of the *argentier* ("*"multum eumdem Argentarium diligebat"*").[3] Those assisting Coeur in Rome included Nicholas V's successor as pope, Calixtus III, and Guillaume de Varye, who had fled France after Coeur's arrest, Jean de Village, and Hugo and Antoine Noir, others of Coeur's business associates. Coeur received permission from Calixtus III to have a small armed guard around him in Rome as he feared attack by henchmen of enemies such as Otto Castellani. Because of the withdrawal from France of some of Coeur's assets by his closest associates such as Guillaume de Varye and the management of his investments by Jean de Village from his location in Marseille, Coeur had funds and could maintain a certain station in life. Rumor had it that Coeur had access to more than 60,000 *écus*, perhaps sequestered from Dauvet's efforts at confiscation. It was said that he could still live honorably, benefiting from his foreign trade.

Coeur was a guest of the papacy, and Pope Calixtus was committed to the idea of a crusade against Turkist expansion in the Levant. Coeur's status as exile may have given him little choice when the pope requested his participation in the crusade. The pope needed Coeur's assistance, and he was hardly in a position to refuse. However, Coeur was clearly still enough of a man of action to seek additional adventures. Moreover, his decision to participate in the papal crusade against Rhodes suggests that he shared the general sentiments of western Christiandom regarding the expansion of Muslim rule in the Mediterranean world. There may have been other rea-

---

[2] A Venetian ducat, a gold coin minted since 1284, was worth 28 *s.* 9 *d. tournois* in 1470 and thus was almost on a par with the écu at 30 s. t. in 1450.

[3] Mollat, 315.

sons, as well. Coeur had earlier, in a letter of 1447 to royal ambassadors in the affairs of Genoa, spoken of himself as indispensable to
the conquest of the Holy Grail.[4] Whatever the interpretation of this
statement, whether reflecting a spiritual commitment, simple self-ag-
grandizement, or realistic pragmatism tied to Genoese politics and
French ambitions, his comment suggests that he saw himself as a man
with a mission. Western Christiandom was distressed by the fall of
Constantinople to the Turks on 29 May 1453.[5] Further, Coeur's desire to re-create a commercial enterprise for himself in the Mediterranean, something which he had begun to do out of Marseille with
the assistance of Jean de Village, and with the business associates he
had around him in Rome, helps explain this decision. The Turkish
conquest of Constantinople represented a threat to any such enterprise. The Turkish leader, Mehmed II, had an army of hundreds of
thousands of men, cannon and numerous galleys that threatened
western commerce. Crusades to preserve Mediterranean trade interests would become a leitmotif of the early modern era. Mehmed also
had tremendous ambition for further expansion, even as far as Rome.
There is no reason to assume that Coeur saw his mercantile career at
an end, not even his French career, if he harbored dreams of returning
to France after a royal pardon. The French tradition of letters of royal
remission of crimes was one from which he (in regard to monetary
fraud) and many others in late medieval France had already benefited. He might do so again. Thus, Coeur's decision to crusade can be
explained by contemporary circumstances. He poured his energies
into the enterprise. There was also a venerable crusade tradition in
France that deserves exploration by way of background. Crusading
fervor had long propelled people from these lands to journey to the
Near East. Along the way, there is more to discover about Jacques
Coeur's nature and orientation.

The concept of crusade had evolved considerably in Europe
since its first emergence as a powerful spiritual and material fusion of pilgrimage and holy war in the preaching of Pope Urban
II in 1095 at Clermont, in central France. From the late twelfth
century, with the western conquest of Constantinople in 1204,
and certainly from the time of Innocent III's early thirteenth-

---

[4] Mollat, Annexes 3, II: 377–8.

[5] This is the date, as well, of Coeur's condemnation by the king.

century crusade in the south of France against Albigensian heretics, who were Christians, not Muslims, the crusade had become a tool in the hands of the popes. It was used in western Europe at times for religious purposes but also for political ends, as the crusades of thirteenth-century popes against Emperor Frederick II of Hohenstaufen (1215–1250) demonstrated. However, the older concept of crusade as a weapon against infidels had not died out. King Louis IX's (1226–1270) first crusade in 1248 was certainly an enterprise aspiring to the same goals as those of the first crusade (1095–1099).

Crusading fervor had been firmly implanted in Champagne in northeastern France even before the Levantine crusades, when noble families from that region joined the *Reconquista* efforts in Spain in the eleventh century. Men of the center and the north of France owed their Mediterranean contacts, if they had any, to the crusade experience. The involvement of many from these regions, and from Champagne in particular, contributed to the evolution of the Champagne fairs in the twelfth, thirteenth, and early fourteenth centuries as the international marketplace of western Europe.

Agricultural fairs in Champagne can be traced back in the written record into the eleventh century, but by the end of the twelfth century Italians were frequenting the fairs, and they had taken on a more international flavor in products as well as participants. The first organized, truly integrated system of mercantile exchange on a Europe-wide scale developed at the fairs. Here the fine wool products of northern France and the Low Countries were exchanged for the spices, drugs, exotic fruits and nuts, and luxury fabrics of the Mediterranean world. The crusades had a role in stimulating the demand upon which the fairs were built. Some crusaders stayed in the Near East and took part in the founding of the crusader principalities, but many returned to Europe, bringing back with them newly acquired tastes for goods to which they had been exposed in the eastern Mediterranean. Europeans needed an export such as fine quality wool cloth, expensive enough to cover at least part of the cost of these eastern products, which could be supplemented by the export of raw materials and precious metals, at first gold and then increasingly silver, as the Middle Ages wore on.

Though the Champagne fairs had declined by the mid-fourteenth century, men of central France like Coeur retained a fascination for the Near East and a crusading zeal that was akin to the early phase of the crusades. The fact that few crusades were actually orchestrated after the end of the thirteenth century did not prevent kings and great lords from taking the vow to crusade. Practical considerations at home in Europe interfered more often than not with the execution of their crusade vows, but crusade planning continued to be a drain on royal treasuries.

With a lull in the Hundred Years War, the court of the young Charles VI was a fertile place for crusade ideas in the 1390s, and Charles himself hoped to convince Richard II of England to join with him in a crusade to free the Holy Land, once the Great Schism of the church was resolved. Philippe de Mézières, the tutor of Charles VI, was instrumental in promoting the crusade to his pupil. Mézières even created a crusading order, the **New Order of the Passion**, to which nobles from both England and France adhered. Furthermore, efforts by figures such as the duke of Bourbon in a crusade to Al-Mahdiya in Tunisia in 1390, or the Prussian exploits of the earl of Derby in 1390 and 1392, stimulated additional crusade interest. Charles VI initiated planning for a crusade which he, his brother Louis, the duke of Orléans, and John of Gaunt would lead. Philip the Bold, duke of Burgundy, the king's youngest uncle, was active in raising funds. King Sigismund of Hungary was to provide an army. The Venetians committed naval forces, and the Roman pope Boniface IX authorized the preaching of the crusade. His Avignon counterpart, Benedict XIII, did the same.

By 1396, as so often with these ambitious endeavors, the shape of the crusade had been transformed, this time into a Burgundian affair with some knights from other French principalities. The major participants included Jean de Boucicaut, Philippe d'Artois, Jean de Vienne, and Enguerrand de Coucy. Drawing on much previous crusade experience, the combined western forces of Burgundians and French, along with Hungarian troops, met an Ottoman army at Nicopolis under Sultan Bayezid, who had been forced to relax his siege of Constantinople as a result of pressure from the western advance into Bulgarian territory. Here the classic French tactical mistake of Courtrai (1302), Crécy (1346), and Poitiers

(1356), the misuse of cavalry, was repeated as the western knights encountered Turkish infantry, who exhausted the knights before they engaged the Ottoman cavalry. The latter then dealt a fatal blow. Western and Hungarian losses were heavy. Jean de Vienne and Guillaume de la Trémoille, the marshal of Burgundy, were killed, and Jean de Boucicaut, Enguerrand de Coucy, Philippe d'Artois, Jean de Nevers (the future duke of Burgundy John the Fearless), and others were captured.

The crusade to Nicopolis was a fiasco from which Anglo-French collaborative efforts would not recover, but the Burgundian commitment remained firm. The future duke of Burgundy, John the Fearless, stopped over at Rhodes on his way home after being ransomed, making contacts with the Hospitallers, which would have consequences for his son Charles the Good's exploits in the 1440s. There was a revival of crusade enthusiasm against the Turks in the 1430s in Europe. The Council of Basel had discussed assistance to the Greeks in 1434 and 1437. Later, the Greeks would turn more directly to Pope Eugenius IV in 1439 in negotiations for the reunion of the eastern Greek and western Latin churches. However, the crusade plan encountered difficulties with the appointment of the antipope Felix V at the Council of Basel in 1439 and the suspicions that Pope Eugenius' actions were merely a ploy for money and prestige. In the end Eugenius' problems at home, in the form of threats against papal territory from the lord of Milan, Filippe Maria Visconti, and rivalry for the throne among the Hungarians, undermined the crusade efforts. The crusade idea stalled again in the late 1430s, when the rhythm of Jacques Coeur's activities was accelerating, but it did not go away.

Coeur's orientation remained Mediterranean throughout his life and culminated in his actual participation on crusade. Long before, it is likely that he was aware of papal projects of crusade and of Burgundian enthusiasm for a crusade revival in the 1430s and 1440s. Coeur's commitment to the Church and to the pope is perhaps nowhere better illustrated than in his last adventure, his participation, while a fugitive in exile from France, on the Rhodes crusade of 1456, organized by the papacy.

Burgundy remained the repository for crusade enthusiasm in the early fifteenth century. From time to time the Burgundian navy concentrated resources in the Mediterranean arena and on the crusade idea that so preoccupied Duke Philip the Good. However, the Burgundians had northern maritime concerns, as well, in the English Channel and North Sea vis-à-vis the English and the German Hansa. A Burgundian invasion of England had actually been planned in 1384–87, with pitiful results. Trade between Flanders and England then became an overriding preoccupation. There followed a lengthy period of little Burgundian naval activity (1387–1435) until the abortive siege of Calais in 1436. However, in the mid-1430s, the attention of the duke of Burgundy turned to the crusading efforts mentioned earlier. A first Burgundian reconnaissance trip to the Near East occurred in 1421. Then, in 1432, Bertrandon de la Broquière, who wrote of his encounter with Coeur in Damascus, went to the Near East for additional reconnaissance, along with other Burgundian nobles at the urging of Philip the Good, who wished to avenge the defeat of his father, John the Fearless, at Nicopolis. Philip the Good then in 1438 directed the construction of a Burgundian fleet. The Burgundians were present with ships in the eastern Mediterranean from 1441 to 1468 for the purpose of combating the Muslims. In May 1441, Burgundian ships were sent to assist the Hospitallers in Rhodes, which would be successfully defended in 1444. With the accession of Mehmed II to the Ottoman throne, Ottoman military prospects improved. Constantinople, the eastern Roman and then Byzantine capital, fell to the Turks on 29 May 1453, marking the end of the eastern Roman Empire.

The fall of Constantinople occasioned much dismay in the west. Pope Nicholas V promulgated a crusading bull against the Turks on 30 September 1453. To stimulate interest within Europe the crusade enthusiast Duke Philip the Good of Burgundy held his famous **Feast of the Pheasant** in February 1454 in Lille. Some two hundred Burgundian nobles took vows to follow their duke. There were other heads of state interested in crusade as well, Alfonso V of Aragon and Naples and Emperor Frederick III of Germany among them. Nicholas V's successor Calixtus III was a Catalan, also committed to the crusade. Appeals made to Charles VII seem to have fallen on deaf ears. For the enthusiastic the strategy remained the same. Get the Hungarians and the Albanians to resist the Turks and bring in the west with naval forces. By late spring 1456, thanks to many papal efforts and much economic turmoil, 16 galleys, worth 150,000 ducats, were armed. This was the force with which Coeur sailed to the eastern Mediterranean on 11 June 1456. (See map on p. 23.)

That Coeur was caught up in this enterprise is not surprising given his region of origin, his involvement in the Mediterranean, his close relations with the popes, and the fact that he was in exile in Rome at the time that Calixtus III organized the crusade effort. At 55 or 60 he still had the energy and enthusiasm for large enterprises. A fugitive from his native land and without responsibilities, he was free to risk his life. His wife was dead, and his children were adults, and with the exception of Ravand, well placed. Ravand appears to have followed his father to Rome, though there is no evidence that he took part in the Rhodes crusade. In espousing the crusade, Coeur carried on a tradition of northern and central Frenchmen in the Mediterranean world. He also had the greatest commitment to international trade among the French since the decline of the Champagne fairs.

Crusade preparations began under Pope Nicholas V but were interrupted abruptly by his death on 24 March 1455. His successor, Pope Calixtus III, at age 77, was himself fixated on the crusade. The pope apparently dealt with most business in singularly terse fashion, but he took time for crusade planning. Calixtus III published a crusading bull on 15 May 1455 that dealt with crusade financing. The crusade was preached in Italy, at Venice, Milan, and Bologna. Then on 8 September Calixtus extended a broader appeal to western Christiandom, appointing two cardinals, a Frenchman, Alain de Coëtivy, and a Spaniard, John of Carvajal, to preach the crusade, and Petro d'Urrea to organize a fleet at Ostia. The crusade effort vastly outstripped the financial resources of the papacy. Coeur, with his talents in finance and his people skills, could be of help. He was invited, along with other talented men, to participate in the crusade enterprise, but in what capacity is unclear. After the fact, his children wished to paint a glorious image of their father. The obituary book of Bourges cathedral called him the "general captain" of the crusade. The papal chancellery made notations of him as "expert for preparing the crusade," a vague title of considerably less magnitude.[6] Coeur is

---

[6] Heers, 216.

noted as having been in Provence along with the French cardinal, Alain de Coëtivy, on 17 September 1455, at which time Coeur put two ships at the disposition of the crusade. The cardinal and Coeur were to engage the religious orders in the enterprise and in the publicity efforts. Coeur apparently visited Provence to recruit personnel to preach the crusade in France, England, Savoy, the Dauphiné, and Flanders and to assist Pope Calixtus' financing efforts. Coeur and Coëtivy were to collect taxes for the enterprise in the form of tithes. Coeur was also charged with the recruitment of maritime personnel for part of the crusade fleet assembling in Provence. Given Coeur's past experience in Provence, the establishment early on of Jean de Village in Marseille as Coeur's representative, and the transfer of the base of Coeur's Mediterranean operations to Marseille from Montpellier in the late 1440s, he was an ideal candidate for these papal responsibilities. These activities of Coeur recall his actions on behalf of the king of France. In fact, Coeur seems simply to have transferred his allegiance to the papacy and re-created himself in the role of *argentier*/commission agent. He may have felt that to excel on behalf of the papacy could aid his cause of reinstatement in the good graces of the French king. But nowhere is he mentioned as commanding crusade ships. Cardinal Aloiso Trevisano, who was patriarch of Aquileia in southern Italy, took charge of the crusade fleet as "general governor and captain."[7]

When a first squadron of ships departed from Ostia on 23 September 1455, two of the ships were listed as galleys of Jacques Coeur. The two galleys in question appear to have left the crusade at Syracuse in Sicily for unknown reasons. With a leadership role, the details of which remain obscure, Coeur and his close associate and former galley captain, Guillaume Gimart, took part in this maritime adventure, likely departing in spring 1456 with a second fleet of ships. There were some additions to the papal fleet at a slightly later date. Arriving first at Rhodes, the fleet then moved around the Aegean, from Chios to other islands, with the crusaders doing little more than effectuating a presence against the Turks. Fortune turned against Coeur anew in the fall of 1456 when Gimart was killed, and he himself was seriously wounded. Deposited

---

[7] Heers, 217.

on the eastern Mediterranean island of Chios where the fleet was to winter, he may have written a last appeal to Charles VII, imploring him to provide for his children.[8] Such a gesture would have been consistent with his desire to regain the king's grace. Coeur died on 25 November 1456. He was buried on Chios in the Cordelier (Franciscan) church. A visitor to the island in 1501 made reference to his tomb in the apse of the church that later Turkish occupation destroyed; his grave has since disappeared.[9] The attempt on the part of Coeur's children to pay homage to his crusader exploits during their rehabilitation efforts speaks to a natural filial desire to recognize a parent but also to the prestige with which crusading was still viewed in the later fifteenth century in France. His children were undoubtedly interested, too, in recovering their father's fortune and in restoring the family name.

Coeur's involvement in the crusade enterprise at the end of his life is consistent with his career-long focus on the Mediterranean world. From the mid-1430s, the Mediterranean again became a focus for Burgundian crusading ambitions. With a far more subtle agenda, Coeur made it a focus for France as well, by venturing east. Driven by a desire to create a direct route of supply of spices for French markets from the Near East and Muslim sources, Coeur was prepared to negotiate with Islam; in his incarnation as crusader he was propelled to combat its expansion. His actions reflect the ambiguity of European responses in regard to the Muslims in the fifteenth century. From hindsight, given the future of European commercial development in the Atlantic world and in Asia, with the age of discoveries ahead, Coeur may seem single-minded. However, Europe presents us in the mid-fifteenth century with parallel universes: the Mediterranean world continuing in the vein of previous centuries, with trade and crusade issues only heightened in intensity because of the Ottoman advance in the Near East, and the Atlantic world, one of discovery and new directions, less well known to people of the time. Coeur's Mediterranean orientation, his creation of a galley fleet, and his steadfast pursuit of commercial advantages for the French set the tone for France, in the reigns of Louis XI and François I, and well into the sixteenth century.

---

[8] Kerr, 276.

[9] Heers, 217.

Conclusions

Jacques Coeur's career accomplishments and the vicissitudes he suffered in his fall from power marked the mid-fifteenth century in a unique way. From the office of *argentier*, from his Mediterranean trade, and from his official roles in minting, monetary policy, and taxation, Coeur was able to generate the finances necessary for Charles VII to win the Hundred Years War, funding the king's military operations with hundreds of thousands of *écus*. This contribution has led historians to attribute the French victory to Charles VII, Joan of Arc, and Jacques Coeur. In this effort Coeur assisted in the creation of permanent taxation that permitted a standing army. *Argentier* was the label that "stuck" to Coeur as he also proved remarkably successful at catering to royal and noble tastes. Building upon traditional medieval business techniques, his methods were strikingly innovative in crafting a system of supply that was totally within his control through a network of associates, assistants, and agents.

French historian Jacques Heers has provided an ambitious reinterpretation of Jacques Coeur in a revisionist (1997) study in which he attacked the traditional vision of Coeur as a merchant entrepreneur, formulated most eloquently by Michel Mollat in 1988. Heers argued that Coeur was essentially a royal officer, a state technician whose enterprise was always accomplished with and directed toward furthering the king's fortunes. Coeur cheated along the way, funneling funds to his own personal and family gain and the creation of an enormous personal fortune. Heers denied that Coeur had ever acted as a merchant and was at best in a tradition of "merchants following the court," a designation of palace merchant that implied no independent function. To sustain his theory, Heers adduced a number of arguments. He situated Coeur within a tradition of nobility of the robe, as opposed to the traditional blood nobility, which he dated to the reign of Charles V (1364–1380). In the reign of Charles VII, Heers found numerous parallels to Coeur's career, such as the family of the Juvénal des Ursins, with father Jean I, and illustrious sons Jean II and Guillaume, both of whom were in contact with Coeur. Son Jacques Juvénal was the bishop of Poitiers who had attempted to have Coeur tried as an ecclesiastic. Several of the Juvénal held positions in the *Parlement de Poitiers*, while enjoying careers in the church and in royal administration, with fortune and influence in the king's service. Guillaume became chancellor of France. Wealth and office were part of the equation for the Juvénal des Ursins and for Jacques Coeur.

According to Heers, all that Coeur did, from his involvement at the *Argenterie*, to the mines of the Lyonnais and the Beaujolais, to the positions of tax collector and royal commissioner in Languedoc and as a member of the king's council, reflected the royal functionary that Coeur represented. Heers maintained that the ships purchased or constructed by Coeur were built with royal funds and were always considered "galleys of France," that Coeur's operations in Montpellier were part of a state enterprise, that his involvement in Mediterranean diplomacy was all a matter of negotiations on behalf of the king. There is a good deal of truth to these statements. But these same galleys of France sailed on behalf of Coeur's mercantile interests, however briefly after his arrest, under the direction of Jean de Village out of Marseille, with the profits of their voyages registered to Coeur's account. Coeur's establishment of Jean de Village in Marseille, his use of the port, and his transfer of the center of his Mediterranean operations to a non-French site suggest that he was also working on his own. The galleys continued to enjoy the safe-conducts and support of the king of Aragon-Naples and the papacy after Coeur's arrest. Coeur also had ships at his disposal that he could dedicate to the papal crusade when he was reestablished in Rome. For Michel Mollat and Louise Guiraud, the shifting of Coeur's operations to Marseille only confirmed his identity as merchant. Even if these moves were an early attempt to cover all bases in the event he ran into difficulty in France, they were in place in the 1440s, years before his arrest in 1451. It is more likely that they served his personal commercial ambitions.

The recent disagreement between historians Mollat and Heers about Coeur's identity, whether royal official or merchant, raises issues that are anachronistic for the fifteenth century. Acknowledgment of Coeur's interest in some independent operations, outside his duties as *argentier*, minter, monetary policy consultant, and royal ambassador, does not introduce an anomaly for the Middle Ages. Medieval merchants made money any way they could. Coeur made no distinction between the personal and the political and combined public and private roles. Coeur viewed the business of the king and his own affairs as a continuum, and, indeed, they were intricately intertwined, something which the fifteenth century accepted easily, but which modern historians have more difficulty sorting out. In fact, Coeur's activities cannot be neatly disengaged from royal affairs. While fulfilling his obligations to the king, Coeur often found ways of profiting personally from his official duties. He took some enterprises such as the mines of the Lyonnais on farm for his personal gain. Sometimes his entree into an operation like mining might be through an official role as tax collector. The independent operations of Coeur emerge more clearly after his escape from prison and his relocation in Rome, when he was no longer in the employ of the king of France. However, even here Coeur's means of operation bore similarities to those he used under Charles VII. When Coeur traveled to Marseille on a pontifical mission in regard to the organization of a crusade, he also worked there on his own behalf, reinforcing business contacts. Coeur would appear to slip in and out of official roles easily, whether working for the king or the pope, making the task of assessment of historians particularly difficult as they debate differing conceptions of the essence of Jacques Coeur.

Sources of Coeur's financing included royal revenues that the king assigned to Coeur's projects such as ship construction, as well as his own profits and reinvestments. Coeur must have had the king's ear to convince him that Mediterranean trade was a worthy investment of royal funds in order to procure the luxury goods desired by the court, the royal entourage, and the nobility of France. Royal revenues also underwrote some of Coeur's trade activities destined to stock the *Argenterie*. There is no denying that Coeur was often employed on royal business. It makes sense to see his operations as a kind of cumulation of functions, both public and private, in the way that these domains were frequently intertwined in the Middle Ages. In matters of business, the lines of public and private were not clearly drawn. Coeur himself did not make the sort of distinctions a modern observer would. He said to the king, "All I have is yours."[1] His critics reversed the phrase. To a degree, both statements have a ring of truth. In the fifteenth century there was no reason why Coeur could not be both merchant and *argentier*.

There is support in fifteenth-century documents for the retention of a dual identity for Coeur. His contemporaries called him, "the" *argentier*, or "*argentier du roi*" or "*commissaire du roi*" (king's commissioner), but fifteenth-century texts also spoke of him as a merchant. The Burgundian chronicler Georges Chastellain, in his *Recollection des merveilles advenues en nostre temps*, mixed the official, mercantile, and financial roles for Coeur:

> Then an *argentier* was seen to rise
> By mystery, the highest in the land,
> Merchant and financier,
> Who, by fate, went to die in exile
> After his many good deeds done
> For the king.[2]

Though Jacques Heers was categorical in denying Coeur a modern or early modern persona, as he said, "An early modern man? Certainly not," it seems useful to categorize Coeur as a transitional figure with aspects of the medieval and the early modern in him.[3] In many of his business techniques he was traditional, using methods that had evolved in the course of the thirteenth century. His people skills reflected the local loyalties to one's region that were current in the Middle Ages, yet he participated fully in the new French identification with king and kingdom. For his close associates he recruited men of Bourges, comrades of youth, and then from this nucleus radiated out to create a broader network of contacts. He was versatile in his affairs and in his relationships, connecting with the powerful of his time, even kings and popes. His charisma bound friends and as-

---

[1] D'Escouchy, II: 286; Mollat, 238.

[2] Chastellain, *Oeuvres*, VII: 190–1; Clément, I: XXVIII–XXIX, note 2.

[3] Heers, 228: "Un homme moderne? Certainement pas." For the French the early modern era is "la période moderne." The modern period is "la période contemporaine."

sociates in good times and in the face of enormous danger. Coeur was remarkably ambitious and desired riches at all cost, but his energy and talents equalled his ambitions. In his peripatetic management style and the integration of services to link supply and demand, he was perhaps unique in any era.

Coeur's formula of state-funded trade blossomed in the form of mercantilism in the *Ancien Régime*. Institutionally the galleys of France lived on in the Mediterranean world, as did the mining operations he stimulated in the Lyonnais. Coeur's economic orientation and cross-cultural initiatives set the tone for future French actions. In the 1460s, Louis XI supported the "galleys of France" in the spice trade via the intermediary of French ports. François I had a French Mediterranean fleet and at times collaborated with the Ottomans. Under Colbert at the time of Louis XIV, merchants and mercantilism coexisted and merchants operated on their own and for the state. Coeur's mixed service in both official and mercantile capacities would have a brilliant future. The beginnings of these trends were certainly present in the fifteenth century, and a strong argument can be made that Coeur contributed to their emergence.

Coeur's trading activities evoke, in fact, the later efforts of Jean-Baptiste Colbert (1619–1683), Louis XIV's great minister, perhaps nowhere more clearly than in regard to the spice trade monopoly. Colbert was a proponent of mercantilism that he coordinated on behalf of France in a somewhat tardy effort to secure political and economic power overseas. Colbert's French East India Company, founded in 1664, decades after similar English (1600) and Dutch (1602) companies were established, had a monopoly in the Orient in the region for which it had a charter, and only merchants belonging to the company could trade there. Merchant input was important in royal commercial enterprise, and merchants acting with the support of the national monarchy were already foreshadowed in Jacques Coeur. Two centuries earlier, Coeur served in the capacity of merchant acting on behalf of the court and the king. There are no inherent contradictions in the terms *merchant*, *mercantilist*, and *capitalist* that could be applied collectively to one individual like Coeur. In regard to trade, he put in place a process enjoying royal support and planning that would bear fruit in the future. France would, a little late, explore new worlds already crowded with other adventurers: Spanish, Portuguese, Dutch, and English.

The Hundred Years War and the presence of Charles VII's court at Bourges facilitated the penetration of Jacques Coeur from his urban mercantile milieu into royal circles, into finance, and into international commerce. Coeur represented a new breed of royal servant, from commoner origins, ennobled by the king, but still vulnerable to the hostility of the traditional nobility. Most of the fifteenth-century commentators on Coeur were sympathetic to him, recognizing his non-noble origins but admiring his contributions. Most were convinced of his wrongful condemnation. The author Martial d'Auvergne, in his long poem of 1477–1483, *Vigiles de Charles VII*, recounting the reign of Charles VII, broke up the chronicle into lessons; the *Quatrième leçon chantée par Marchandise* evoked Coeur:

> And if certain of them [the merchants]. . .
> Were enriched, does this nevertheless mean
> That one should take them,
> Whether right or wrong,
> Pillage or sell their goods,
> Confiscate them and give them away
> without misjudging?. . .
> Alas, what danger from false accusers,
> Bad boys and drastic reducers,
> Who tell lies to lords
> To undo many good merchants,
> To take their money
> Without hearing them in justice
> Or doing right or reason.
> And then be their adversary
> In a trial,
> And taking judges of their bent and access,
> O what abuse and what horrible excess. . . . [4]

The allusions to Coeur are unmistakable in the references to confiscation and false accusers. Martial d'Auvergne made clear that merchants were in danger of being pillaged of their resources, falsely accused by evil men and lords, improperly tried in justice, with their enemies as judges of their fate. This, he

---

[4] The original text in d'Auvergne, 18–19, is somewhat longer than that quoted by Clément, I: XXX, who condensed the original. I have chosen to translate the shorter text, which makes the author d'Auvergne's points succinctly.

thought, was a matter of terrible abuse and excess. Martial d'Auvergne would have known of what he spoke, as he was a prosecutor at the *Parlement de Paris*.

Jacques Coeur is a fascinating figure as much because of the extent and variety of his activities and of his success as for his limitations and fall from favor. Michel Mollat correctly situated Coeur in his fifteenth-century niche, in claiming that Coeur could not predict the Atlantic future of Europe or the Ottoman triumph in the Near East. He never dreamed of new worlds, from what is known of him. Though an *argentier* concerned with the supply of markets, he did not entertain the notion of a direct sea route to the products of South Asia and the Far East.

The paradox of Coeur's non-involvement in the age of exploration, noted by Jean Favier and Edouard Perroy, can be resolved. Coeur functioned with the tools of his time, that is to say, earlier Italian techniques of commerce and finance, in large measure. There were, of course, certain advances over the thirteenth century by the first half of the fifteenth, in banking, for example, at the Casa di San Giorgio at Genoa, followed by the banking institutions of Barcelona, Majorca, and Valencia, but Coeur did not pattern his financial activities after such innovations. In his spice and luxury trade he never attempted to eliminate Near Eastern Muslim intermediaries. For him it was a matter of negotiating with Islam on behalf of French interests and his own trade, and of substituting his operations for those of the Italians and other European Mediterranean traders. His genius was in the creation of an integrated delivery system for the fruits of his trade.

That Jacques Coeur acquired the baggage of legend after his death should not surprise modern readers. His reputation and his enormous wealth, his power within Europe, his gift for public relations, his association with kings and popes, and his contribution to the end of the Hundred Years War made him a formidable personage before his fall from grace. His arrest and condemnation only served to exaggerate his exploits. His escape from prison and his departure from France, never to set foot again on French shores, brought a cloud of mystery down on his many real deeds that were themselves out of the ordinary for the time. One of the legends attached to Coeur suggests he had carrier pigeons, an Arabic invention, to transfer brief bits of information. Given the vast network of agents and operations that Coeur managed, it is understandable that such a technique might be attached to him. Other myths include Coeur's role as an alchemist. If he had been successful, Charles VII's finances would certainly have profited. Finally, Coeur's death in a distant land on crusade added the final touch to a life that astounded and intrigued contemporaries. In legend Coeur is construed as the crusade leader who, far from dying in Chios, went on to have an illustrious second career in the Near East in Cyprus, supposedly remarrying and having two daughters, who themselves married well and continued the struggle against the Turks. There is no need for legend, however, as the last years of Jacques Coeur's life retain the rhythm and excitement of much of his mature existence, further enhancing his reputation.

A Note on the Sources

All English translations are my own.

I am indebted to centuries of French scholarship on Jacques Coeur in this study. Most recently, the biographical works of Michel Mollat, *Jacques Coeur ou l'esprit d'entreprise au XVe siècle* (Paris: Aubier, 1988), and Jacques Heers, *Jacques Coeur 1400–1456* (Paris: Perrin, 1997), provide diametrically opposed interpretations of this elusive fifteenth-century figure. Of continuing interest is the early twentieth-century study by Louise Guiraud, *Recherches et conclusions nouvelles sur le prétendu rôle de Jacques Coeur* (Paris: Picard, 1900). This study also appeared as an issue of the *Mémoires de la Société. Archéologique de Montpellier*, 2nd series, II (1902): 1–169. These historians built on a long tradition of scholarly interest in Jacques Coeur, beginning in his own time period with the commentaries of chroniclers and poets, particularly following his downfall.

The evidence for a study of Jacques Coeur remains scattered in archives in France and in the western Mediterranean world. A major source is the *Journal du Procureur Dauvet*, the confiscation records after Coeur's condemnation, the manuscript of which (KK 328) is at the Archives Nationales; it was published by Michel Mollat et al., *Les affaires de Jacques Coeur. Journal du Procureur Dauvet*, 2 vols. (Paris: Librairie Armand Colin, 1952–1953). For several years after the arrest of Coeur, the royal prosecutor Jean Dauvet traveled throughout France interrogating people in an effort to confiscate Jacques Coeur's property to pay off debts to the king and fines levied by royal judicial judgment against Coeur. Dauvet was only partly successful in identifying Coeur's holdings but has left the historian a remarkable journal detailing his travels and his actions at the time of Coeur's escape. Collections of documents related to the lawsuit against Coeur survive in several manuscripts in French archives, including the Bibliothèque de l'Institut in Paris and the Bibliothèque des Quatre Piliers in Bourges. There are several manuscripts recording the letter of marque proceedings of the 1440s, including ms. 207 of the Bibliothèque Municipale of Montpellier.

Michel Mollat collected and edited 12 missives of Jacques Coeur that can be identified as his correspondence and included them in his biography as Annexes 3. "Lettres de Jacques Coeur," 375–92. Many of the documents discussed in the present book are based on these documents. There may be a few other pieces scattered in French archives, but it seems safe to say that from Jacques Coeur's own hand there remains very little. Coeur does not seem to have kept elaborate records and may not have maintained significant accounts, though it is difficult to say for certain since materials related to his operations were spirited out of France by his closest colleagues after his arrest. We do not know what level of education Coeur had. A few documents carry his signature: an elaborate but somewhat awkward rendering of "Ja Cuer" with a multi-lobed sign. Pierre Clément, *Jacques Coeur et Charles VII*, 2 vols. (Paris: Librairie de Guillaumin et Cie, 1853), provided discussion of and quotations regarding Jacques Coeur by many of Coeur's contemporaries, chroniclers and poets alike. I have consulted printed editions of the fifteenth-century works cited.

Quotations from fifteenth-century chronicle authors have been footnoted in secondary sources, including Mollat, Heers, and Clément, that will be accessible to the reader. The original works from which citations have been taken are by no means all-inclusive of fifteenth-century mentions of Jacques Coeur, but they provide illustrations of how the man and his actions were perceived. The following list provides abbreviations to the Dauvet journal, the cited chronicle authors, and pertinent secondary sources, as found in brief footnotes to the text:

Printed Sources

Basin, *Charles VII et Louis XI* — Basin, Thomas (1412–1491). *Histoire des règnes de Charles VII et Louis XI.* 4 vols. Paris: J. Renouard, 1855–1859.

Basin, *Charles VII* — Basin, Thomas. *Histoire de Charles VII*, ed. and trans. Charles Samaran. 2 vols. Paris: Société d'édition "Les Belles Lettres," 1933–1944.

Chastellain, *Oeuvres* — Chastellain, Georges (1405/15–1475). *Oeuvres.* 8 v. Brussels: F. Heussner, 1863–1866.

Chastellain, *Bocace* — Chastellain, Georges. *Le temple de Bocace.* Berne: Francke, 1988.

D'Auvergne — D'Auvergne, Martial (1430/35–1508). *Les vigiles de la mort du roy Charles VII*, vol. IV. (also *Les poësies de Martial de Paris, dit d'Auvergne.*) Paris: A. U. Coustelier, 1724.

Dauvet I and II — Mollat, Michael et al., *Les affaires de Jacques Coeur. Journal du Procureur Dauvet*, 2 vols. Paris: Librairie Armand Colin, 1952–1953.

D'Escouchy — D'Escouchy, Mathieu (1420–1482). *Chronique de Mathieu d'Escouchy*, ed. G. du Fresne de Beaucourt. New ed. Paris: Mme. Ve J. Renouard, 1863–1864.

Du Clercq — Du Clercq, Jacques (ca.1420–1501). *Mémoires de Jacques Du Clercq, escuier, sieur de Beauvoir en Ternois, commençant en 1448, et finissant en 1467.* Paris: 1836–1839.

Villon — Villon, François (1431–1463). *Le testament.*, ed. Jérôme Vérain. Paris: Mille et une nuits, 2000.

Secondary Sources

Clément
Clément, Pierre. *Jacques Coeur et Charles VII*. 2 vols. Paris: Librairie de Guillaumin et Cie, 1853.

Guiraud
Guiraud, Loise. *Recherches et conclusions nouvelles sur le prétendu rôle de Jacques Coeur*. Paris: Picard, 1900.

Heers
Heers, Jacques. *Jacques Coeur 1400–1456*. Paris: Perrin, 1997.

Kerr
Kerr, Albert Boardman. *Jacques Coeur. Merchant Prince of the Middle Ages*. London, New York: Charles Scribner's Sons, 1927.

Marinesco, "Du nouveau"
Marinesco, Constantin. "Du nouveau sur Jacques Coeur," *Mélanges d'histoire du moyen âge dédiés à la mémoire de Louis Halphen*. Paris: Presses Universitaires de France, 1951, 491–500.

Marinesco, "Nouveaux"
Marinesco, Constantin. "Nouveaux renseignements sur Jacques Coeur," *Eventail de l'histoire vivante. Hommage à Lucien Febvre*. Vol. II. Paris: Librairie Armand Colin, 1953: 163–74.

Mérindol
De Mérindol, Christian. "L'Emblématique des demeures et chapelles de Jacques Coeur. Une nouvelle lecture. La Grande Loge de Montpellier et les monuments de Bourges," *Actes du 110e Congrès national des Sociétés savantes*, II: *Recherches sur l'histoire de Montpellier et du Languedoc*. Paris, 1986, 153–78.

Mollat   Mollat, Michel. *Jacques Coeur ou l'esprit d'entreprise au XVe siècle*. Paris: Aubier, 1988.

Mollat, "Une équipe."   Mollat, Michel. "Une équipe: les commis de Jacques Coeur" *Eventail de l'histoire vivante. Hommage à Lucien Febvre*. Vol. II. Paris: Armand Colin, 1953, 175–85.

Very helpful reference tools are the two encyclopedias, *Trade, Travel, and Exploration in the Middle Ages*, ed. John Block Friedman and Kristen Mossler Figg (New York: Garland, 2000), and *Medieval France*, ed. William W. Kibler, Grover A . Zinn, Lawrence Earp, and John Bell Henneman (New York: Garland, 1995). The following selected bibliographical suggestions for further reading are organized by chapters.

Chapter 1—By way of general background, specifically on medieval France, the general text by Claude Gauvard, *La France au Moyen Age du Ve au XVe siècle* (Paris: Presses Universitaires de France, 1996) is very useful, as are Elizabeth Hallam, *Capetian France, 987–1328* (Longman: London and New York, 1980); Peter Lewis, *Later Medieval France: The Polity* (New York: St. Martin's Press, 1968); and Bernard Guenée, *L'Occident aux XIVe et XVe siècles, les Etats* (Paris: Presses Universitaires de France, 1971; new ed., 1991).

On the Hundred Years War, there are many works. Among the most useful in English are Christopher Allmand, *The Hundred Years War, England and France at War c. 1300–c. 1450* (Cambridge: Cambridge University Press, 1988); Edouard Perroy, *The Hundred Years War* (New York: Capricorn Books, 1965); Jonathan Sumption, *The Hundred Years War. Vol. I: Trial by Battle* (Philadelphia: The University of Pennsylvania Press, 1990) and *The Hundred Years War. Vol. II: Trial by Fire* (Philadelphia: The University of Pennsylvania Press, 1999). See also Richard W. Kaeuper. *War, Justice and Public Order. England and France in the Later Middle Ages* (Oxford: Oxford University Press, 1988).

On Joan of Arc, see Bonnie Wheeler and Charles T. Wood, *Fresh Verdicts on Joan of Arc* (New York: Garland, 1996); Georges and Andrée Duby *Les procès de Jeanne d'Arc* (Paris:

Gallimard, 1995); Régine Pernoud, *Joan of Arc by Herself and Her Witnesses* (Lanham, New York, London: Scarborough House, new edition, 1994). See also the evaluation of Joan by Kelly de Vries, *Joan of Arc. A Military Leader* (Stroud, Gloucestershire: Sutton Publishing, 1999).

On the later medieval kings, Françoise Autrand's two biographies in French, *Charles V* (Paris: Fayard, 1994) and *Charles VI* (Paris: Fayard, 1986), are essential. On Charles VII, Philippe Bully, *Charles VII "Le roi des merveilles"* (Paris: Tallander, 1994). For the study of Jacques Coeur and Charles VII, the old work by Clément, *Jacques Coeur et Charles VII*, as noted above, is invaluable. For an understanding of the evolution of royal sentiment and politics, see Colette Beaune, *The Birth of an Ideology; Myths and Symbols of Nation in Late Medieval France* (Berkeley: University of California Press, 1991), translation of *Naissance de la nation France* (Paris: Gallimard, 1984); Jacques Krynen, *L'Empire du roi. Idées et croyances politiques en France, XIIIe-XVe siècle* (Paris: Gallimard, 1993); Olivier Guillot, Albert Rigaudière, and Yves Sassier, *Pouvoirs et institutions dans la France médiévale*, 2 vols. (Paris: Librairie Armand Colin, 1994).

On the medieval beginnings of exploration, see Felipe Fernández-Armesto, *Before Columbus: Exploration and Colonisation from the Mediterranean to the Atlantic, 1229–1492)* (Houndmills, Basingstoke, Hampshire, and London, 1987); William D. Phillips, Jr. and Carla Rahn Phillips, *The Worlds of Christopher Columbus* (Cambridge: Cambridge University Press, 1992); Pierre Chaunu, *L'Expansion européenne du XIIIe au XVe siècle*, 3rd ed. (Paris: Presses Universitaires de France, 1995); Jean Favier, *Gold and Spices: The Rise of Commerce in the Middle Ages*, trans. Caroline Higgitt (New York: Holmes and Meier, 1998); Jean-Paul Roux, *Les Explorateurs au Moyen Age* (Paris: Fayard, 1985). On world history personalities, see Ken Wolf, *Personalities and Problems: Interpretive Essays in World Civilizations* (New York: McGraw Hill, 1994).

On medieval maritime matters, see Michel Mollat, *La vie quotidienne des gens de mer à la fin du Moyen Age* (Paris, 1983), and *Le commerce maritime normand* (Paris, 1952). See also Frederic C. Lane, *Venice. A Maritime Republic* (Baltimore: Johns Hopkins University Press, 1973).

Chapter 2—On Jacques Coeur himself, the works by Michel Mollat are pertinent, in particular, his above-mentioned biography, *Jacques Coeur ou l'esprit d'entreprise*. Jacques Heers' *Jacques Coeur* represents the most recent interpretation of Coeur, as mentioned above. See also Claude Poulain, *Jacques Coeur ou les Rêves concrétisés* (Paris: Fayard, 1982); H. de Man, *Jacques Coeur. Argentier du roy* (French trans. Paris: Tardy, 1951); Jean-Yves Ribault, "Jacques Coeur 'natif de Bourges,'" *Cahiers archéologique et historique du Berry* 14 (1968): 67–76, and Ribault, "Les biens immobiliers de Jacques Coeur à Bourges," *Mémoires de l' Union des Sociétés Savantes de Bourges* 9 (1961–1962): 41–66. Still provocative is the old work of Louise Guiraud, *Recherches et conclusions*. There is very little in English on Jacques Coeur, aside from Albert Boardman Kerr, *Jacques Coeur: Merchant Prince of the Middle Ages* (London, New York: Charles Scribner's Sons, 1927) and the historical novel by Thomas B. Costain, *The Moneyman* (Garden City, N. Y.: Doubleday, 1947).

On daily life and childhood during the period of Jacques Coeur, see Roger Virgoe, ed., *Private Life in the Fifteenth Century* (New York: Weidenfeld & Nicolson, 1989); David Nicholas, *The Domestic Life of the Medieval City. Women, Children and Families in Fourteenth Century Ghent* (Lincoln, NE 1985); Compton Reeves, *Pleasures and Pastimes in Medieval England* (Phoenix Mill: Alan Sutton Publishing, 1995); P. Metcalf, "Living Over the Shop in the City of London," *Architectural History* 27 (1984): 96–103; and Kathryn L. Reyerson, "The Adolescent Apprentice/Worker in Medieval Montpellier," *Journal of Family History* 17 (1992): 353–70. Of particular value for the study of late medieval childhood is Barbara A. Hanawalt, *Growing Up in Medieval London: The Experience of Childhood in History* (New York, Oxford: Oxford University Press, 1993).

Chapter 3—For further reading see Mollat, Heers, and Guiraud, who all treat, in detail, the roles of Coeur as a royal functionary. For the specific case of salt, see Michel Mollat, "Le sel dans les affaires de Jacques Coeur," *Le Roi, le marchand et le sel*, ed. J. Cl. Hocquet, *Coll. Arc et Senans 1986* (Paris, 1987), and "Speculations de Jacques Coeur sur le sel du Languedoc," *Bulletin philologique et historique C. T. H. S. 1958 (1959)*: 206–210. See also Jean-Yves Ribault, "Un project de lettres de rémission fiscale en faveur des habitants des diocèses d'Agde, comté de Pézenas et seigneurie de Montagnac en 1440," *Actes du 110e Congrès national des Sociétés savantes, II: Recherches sur l'histoire de Montpellier et du Languedoc* (Paris, 1986): 141–52.

On money and minting, see Etienne Fournial, *Histoire monétaire de l'Occident médiéval* (Paris: Fernand Nathan, 1970), and Harry A. Miskimin, *Money and Power in Fifteenth-Century France* (New Haven and London: Yale University Press, 1984).

On fashion in the late Middle Ages, see Françoise Piponnier and Perrine Mane, *Dress in the Middle Ages*, trans. Caroline Beamish (New Haven: Yale University Press, 1997).

On Colbert and mercantilism, see R. R. Palmer, *A History of the Modern World* (New York: Alfred A. Knopff, 1965), and Glenn Ames, *Colbert, Mercantilism, and the French Quest for Asian Trade* (DeKalb: Northern Illinois University Press, 1996). Chapter 4—For a general background on the economy in medieval Europe, see Robert S. Lopez, *The Commercial Revolution of the Middle Ages, 950–1350* (Cambridge: Cambridge University Press, 1976) and *The Birth of Europe* (New York: M. Evans, 1966); Harry A. Miskimin, *The Economy of Early Renaissance Europe, 1300–1460* (Cambridge: Cambridge University Press, 1975); N. J. G. Pounds, *An Economic History of Medieval Europe*, 2nd ed. (London and New York: Longman, 1994). Mollat, Heers, and Guiraud deal in depth with the Mediterranean trade of Jacques Coeur.

On Coeur's involvement in the south of France and in Mediterranean trade, see Louis J. Thomas, *Montpellier ville marchande. Histoire Economique et Sociale de Montpellier des origines à 1870* (Montpellier: Libraire Vallat, Libraire Coulet, 1936); Jean Combes, *Montpellier et le Languedoc au Moyen-Age, Mémoires de la Société Archéologique de Montpellier* 20 (Montpellier, 1990); Guy Romestan, "Les hommes d'affaires de Perpignan dans le royaume de Naples à l'époque d'Alfonse le Magnanime," *IXe Congrès historique de la Couronne d'Aragon-Naples*, 1973, vol. II: *La Corona de*

Aragon e il Mediterraneo (Naples, 1982): 81–106, and "Quelques relations d'affaires de Jacques Coeur à Perpignan," *Annales du Midi* 79 (1967): 19–28; Bernard Doumerc, "Les marchands du Midi à Alexandrie au XVe siècle," *Annales du Midi* 97 (1985): 269–84; Anne-Catherine Marin, "L'Immigration à Montpellier au XVe siècle d'après les registres d'habitanage (1422–1442)," *Actes du 110e Congrès national des Sociétés savantes*, II: *Recherches sur l'histoire de Montpellier et du Languedoc* (Paris, 1986): 99–123. See also the general study of Montpellier, *Histoire de Montpellier*, ed. Gérard Cholvy (Toulouse: Privat, 1984).

Both Mollat and Heers in their biographies discuss matters relating to Coeur's entourage. See also Michel Mollat, "Une équipe: les commis de Jacques Coeur," *Eventail de l'histoire vivante. Hommage à Lucien Febvre* II (Paris: Armand Colin, 1953): 175–85. The letter requesting assistance from Jean de Village was reproduced by Mollat, *Jacques Coeur*, 391–2, from the edition by Clément, *Jacques Coeur et Charles VII*, II: 192–4.

On the shape of Italian medieval business, see Yves Renouard, *Les hommes d'affaires italiens du moyen âge* (Paris: Librairie Armand Colin, 1968); Raymond de Roover, *The Rise and Decline of the Medici Bank*, 1397–1494 (New York: W. W. Norton, 1966). On business and banking, see *The Dawn of Modern Banking* (New Haven: Yale University Press, 1979); also Kathryn L. Reyerson, *Business, Banking and Finance in Medieval Montpellier* (Toronto: The Pontifical Institute of Mediaeval Studies, 1985), and *The Art of the Deal: Intermediaries of Trade in Medieval Montpellier* (Leiden: E. J. Brill, 2002).

Chapter 5—On fifteenth-century finance, see Michel Mollat, "Les opérations financières de Jacques Coeur," *Revue de la Banque* 17 (Brussels, 1954): 125–42. On the accounts of an associate of Coeur, see Liberto Valls, "Le livre de comptes de Pierre Colombier, facteur de Jacques Coeur (1444–1445)," *Hommage à Jean Combes (1903–1989). Etudes Languedociennes offertes par ses anciens élèves, collègues et amis* (Montpellier, 1991), 115–21.

Robert Guillot, *Le procès de Jacques Coeur (1451–1457)* (Bourges: Imprimerie Dusser, 1974), provides the text of the condemnation decree against Coeur. Emily Sohmer Tai, "Honor among Thieves: Piracy, Restitution, and Reprisal in Genoa, Venice, and the Crown of Catalonia-Aragon, 1339–1417," (Ph.D. thesis, Harvard University, 1996), has traced the integration of restitution, reprisal, and piracy into the Mediterranean economy in a period just before that of Jacques Coeur. On piracy, see also Robert C. Ritchie, *Captain Kidd and the War against the Pirates* (Cambridge, MA: Harvard University Press, 1986). Other important works include Brigitte Laîné, "Recherches sur le commerce de Jacques Coeur en Languedoc, Roussillon, etc.," *Actes du 91e Congrès National des Sociétés Savantes*, Rennes, 1966; *Bulletin philologique et historique* 1 (1968): 143–56; Guy Romestan, "Quelques relations d'affaires de Jacques Coeur à Perpignan," *Annales du Midi* 79 (1967): 19-28; Constantin Marinesco, "Du nouveau sur Jacques Coeur," *Mélanges d'histoire du moyen âge dédiés à la mémoire de Louis Halphen* (Paris: Presses Universitaires de France, 1951), 491–500; "Nouveaux renseignements sur Jacques Coeur," *Eventail de l'histoire vivante. Hommage à Lucien Febvre*, II (Paris: Librarie Armand Colin, 1953), 163–74; "Jacques Coeur et ses affaires aragonaises, catalanes et napolitaines," *Revue historique* 205 (1951): 224–37.

On the controversial topic of alchemy, see Roger Facon and Jean-Marie Parent, *Gilles de Rais et Jacques Coeur. La conspiration des innocents.* (Paris: Robert Laffont, 1984). See also *Fulcaneli: Master Alchemist. Le Mystère des Cathédrales*, trans. Mary Sworder (Albuquerque: Brotherhood of Life, 1984).

For background on the late medieval church, conciliarism, and schism, see Brian Tierney, *Religion, Law and the Growth of Constitutional Thought, 1150-1650* (Cambridge: Cambridge University Press, 1982), and Antony Black, *Monarchy and Community: Political Ideas in the Later Conciliar Controversy 1430–1450* (Cambridge: Cambridge University Press, 1970).

Chapter 6—On the house of Jacques Coeur in Bourges, see Jean Favière, *L'Hôtel de Jacques Coeur à Bourges* (Paris: Picard and Caisse Nationale des Monuments Historiques et des Sites, 1992), and the pamphlet by Jean-Marie Jenn, "The Palace Jacques-Coeur" (Rennes: Editions Ouest-France/CNMHS, 1991). See also the material on Jacques Coeur in *La Société Ur-*

baine au Moyen Age: Marchands et Métiers, fasc. 6009 (Documentation Photographique, Dossier individuel no. 9, 1974), and Ribault, "Les biens immobiliers de Jacques Coeur à Bourges."

On the holdings of Jacques Coeur in Montpellier, see the study by Guiraud, *Recherches et conclusions,* and Jacques Fabre de Morlhan, "L'Hôtel Nicolas et le séjour de Jacques-Coeur à Montpellier," *Extrait de la Fédération Historique du Languedoc Méditerranéen et du Roussillon* (XXXIXe Congrès–Montpellier, 1966) (Montpellier: Imprimerie Paul Déhan, 1967), 1–15.

New interpretations of decorative details or emblems associated with Jacques Coeur have been offered by Christian de Mérindol. See, for example, "L'Emblématique des demeures et chapelles de Jacques Coeur. Une nouvelle lecture. La Grande Loge de Montpellier et les monuments de Bourges," *Actes du 110e Congrès national des Sociétés savantes,* II: *Recherches sur l'histoire de Montpellier et du Languedoc* (Paris, 1986): 153–78.

Chapter 7—Mollat, Heers, and Guillot provide informative discussion of the accusations and legal proceedings against Jacques Coeur. See also Samuel H. Cuttler, *The Law of Treason and Treason Trials in Later Medieval France* (Cambridge: Cambridge University Press, 1981). I am grateful to Alfred Soman, emeritus of the CNRS (Centre national de la recherche scientifique), for his comments and advice on Coeur's legal difficulties. On efforts to assist Coeur after his arrest and on his trial and condemnation, see Robert Guillot, *Le procès de Jacques Coeur* (Bourges: Imprimerie Dusser, 1974), for the most substantive treatment. Citations of Gérard Machet, Mathieu d'Escouchy, and Georges Chastellain come from Mollat, *Jacques Coeur.* See also Kathryn L. Reyerson, "*Le procès de Jacques Coeur,*" *Les procès politiques (xve–xviie siécle)* (Rome: Ecole française de Rome, forthcoming).

Specifically on the escape of Jacques Coeur from Poitiers, see Mollat et al., *Les affaires de Jacques Coeur,* as noted above. See also Antoine Thomas, "L'Evasion et la mort de Jacques Coeur," *Revue historique* 98 (1908): 72–86.

On Louis XI, see Paul Murray Kendall, *Louis XI . . . "the universal spider . . ."* (New York: W. W. Norton, 1971).

Chapter 8—On the late medieval crusades, see Norman Housley, *The Later Crusades* (Oxford: Oxford University Press,

1992); Harry W. Hazard, *A History of the Crusades*, III: *The Fourteenth and Fifteenth Centuries* (Madison: The University of Wisconsin Press, 1975); Hazard and Norman P. Zacour, VI: *The Impact of the Crusades on Europe* (Madison: The University of Wisconsin Press, 1989); and Jonathan Riley-Smith, *The Crusades: A Short History* (New Haven and London: Yale University Press, 1987). See also Johan Huizinga, *The Autumn of the Middle Ages*, trans. Rodney J. Payton and Ulrich Mammitzsch (Chicago: University of Chicago Press, 1996). On the Burgundian navy, see Jacques Paviot, *La politique navale des ducs de Bourgogne, 1384–1482* (Lille: Presses Universitaires de Lille, 1995).

Glossary

à coeur vaillant rien impossible: for the valiant of heart, nothing is impossible.

Ancien Régime: old regime, a term referring to the seventeenth and eighteenth centuries in France.

argentier: bursar, commission agent, silversmith.

asylum: refuge from legal pursuit.

avoir du poids: term usually applied to spices, literally means having weight, i. e. value.

bailliage: administrative district in France, headed by a bailiff.

Cabochien ordinance: legislation of 1413 mandating administrative reforms in France.

Cabochien revolt: 1413 uprising in Paris, led by butcher Caboche.

cambium: money exchange.

canon law: the common law of the Church.

canonate: office of a cathedral priest.

Chamber of Accounts (*Chambre des comptes*): financial branch of the royal court overseeing the account of the king's ordinary finances from the royal domain.

chancery: writing office.

Capeluche revolt: 1418 uprising in Paris, led by the executioner Capeluche.

commenda: a maritime or land partnership, usually with an investing partner who contributed capital and a traveling partner who contributed labor, with the division of profits, 3/4 for the investing partner and 1/4 for the traveling partner.

Conciliarism: doctrine asserting the superiority of councils over the pope in the governance of the Church.

consul: a representative of the executive branch of municipal government in the south of France and Italy.

consulate: a form of municipal government, common to southern France and Italy in the Middle Ages.

contract: a legally binding engagement with obligations of a monetary, personal, or legal sort.

coquilles St. Jacques: scallop shells, one of Coeur's emblems.

Cordeliers: a French term for the Franciscans.

corsair: privateer whose piracy was authorized by a political power.

Council of Basel: general Church council (1431–1438).

Council of Constance: general Church council (1414–1418).

Cour des aides: financial branch of government with oversight of taxes or extraordinary finances.

d. *(denarius):* a penny or *denier*; a common denomination of medieval coinage.

dauphin: heir to the French throne.

Dominicans: teaching and preaching friars.

dower: rights of a widow over her late husband's property.

dowry: money and/or property that a woman brings to a marriage.

draper: cloth merchant, a prestigious medieval profession.

ducat: Venetian gold coin.

écu, écus: French gold coin.

episcopal: referring to a bishop.

factor: a business agent.

farm: administrative procedure of selling the right to collect a tax or exploit a revenue-producing entity.

Feast of the Pheasant: Burgundian celebration of Duke Philip the Good in Lille in 1454 to encourage crusade enthusiasm and crusading vows.

finances extraordinaires: royal revenues from taxation.

finances ordinaires: revenues from royal domain.

fleur de lys: lily, French royal emblem.

florin: gold coin of France and Italy.

fondaco, fondachi: foreign merchant colony(ies) with extraterritorial rights.

Franciscans: mendicant friars.

gabelle: French salt tax.

galea de mercaderia: commercial galley.

galley: oarred vessel, sometimes equipped with sail.

Gallican: party supporting independence of French Church from papal control.

Golden Fleece, Order of the: late medieval Burgundian knightly order, founded by Duke Philip the Good in 1429.

in utroque jure: in both laws, meaning both civil and canon law.

Jacobins: a French term for the Dominicans.

langue d'oc: language of southern France, "*oc*" meaning "yes."

langue d'oil: language of northern France, "*oil*" meaning "yes."

law of marque: regulations governing reprisal and retribution.

lèse-majesté: treason.

letter of marque: authorization from a political authority to seek reprisal and retribution for wrongs.

lettre de rémission: royal letter of pardon.

l.(libra, librarum): pound(s); a monetary unit of coinage.

lit de justice: important session of *Parlement* with the king present.

l. t. (librarum turonensium or *livres tournois):* pounds *tournois*; French royal coinage of Tours.

loge: commercial exchange.

mark: a unit of weight or value of gold or silver.

menu vair: squirrel pelt.

mercantilism: early modern state-sponsored and state-regulated economic activity, often of a competitive capitalist type.

money of account: system of standardized computation or accounting whereby 12 pennies equal one shilling; 20 shillings equal one pound; thus 240 pennies equal one pound, regardless of actual precious metal content.

more piratico: in the manner of pirates.

nave: central aisle of a church.

nef: in maritime terms a wide, round ship driven by sails; a church nave.

New Order of the Passion: a crusading order.

noblesse d'épee: hereditary blood nobility in France.

noblesse de robe: nobility of the robe (of office), ennobled by the king of France.

Parisis coinage: French royal coinage of Paris.

parlement: a high court, the *Parlement de Paris* was the supreme court of the kingdom of France.

parva barcha: a small boat.

pax mongolica: Mongol peace, referring to safe conditions of travel across Asia under Mongol rule.

pays: homeland.

pays de connaissance: land where one was known and had contacts.

Petit Scel: court of voluntary jurisdiction of medieval Montpellier.

p. t.: petits tournois; French royal coinage of Tours.

Praguerie: 1439–1440 revolt of princes against Charles VII's efforts to outlaw private armies.

Pragmatic Sanction of Bourges: Promulgation of 1438 reestablishing elections for major Church offices, limiting papal influence.

Prince of the Blood: a late term referring to princes related, sometimes distantly, to the royal family.

privateer: pirate authorized by a government; *see* corsair.

procuration (*procuratio*): a delegation of authority through legal representation, with specific or general mandate to act.

procurator (*procurator*): legal representative.

real guerdon: royal guard.

Recettes Générales: French royal accounting organ.

Reconquista: Christian reconquest effort to regain Iberian/Spanish territory from Muslim rule.

registres d'habitanage: registers of inhabitants.

rentes: annuities.

royals *(réaux, regales)*: gold coins.

sceaux rigoureux: French royal courts of voluntary jurisdiction, particularly applicable to the new economy of trade and finance in medieval towns; examples include the court of the wardens of the Champagne fairs, the court of the *Petit Scel* in Montpellier, and the *Cour des Conventions* in Nîmes.

sénéchaussée: French territorial administrative district.

s. t. (sous tournois): shillings *tournois*; French royal coinage of Tours.

taille: tax, tallage on non-noble households and hearths; also a head tax on non-nobles.

Treaty of Troyes: 1420 treaty by which Charles VI willed France to Henry V of England.

Très Riches Heures: devotional book with illustrations by the Limbourg brothers, painters.

Tournois coinage: French royal coinage, broad circulation.

ultramarinis (outremer): beyond the sea.

venality: purchase of office in the *Ancien Régime*.

visiteur général: inspector general.

A Note on
Medieval Money

Silver coinage was the norm from the Carolingian period to the mid-thirteenth century in Europe when gold coinage (for France, royals, florins, and *écus*, among other coins) was reinstituted, alongside silver. Money of account established a standard of equivalence among real coins of different denominations. Real coins, actually minted, must be distinguished from money of account, which was a system of accounting in pounds (*l.* or *livres*), shillings (*s.* or *sous*), and pennies (*d.* or *deniers*), with the equivalencies of 12 pennies (12 *d.*) to one shilling (1 *s.*) and 20 shillings (20 *s.*) or 240 pennies (240 *d.*) to one pound (1 *l.*). No *livres* or *sous* were ever minted; pennies were the main coin in circulation, though large transactions required a coin of higher denomination, and the groat (*gros tournois*), worth 12 to 15 pennies (*d.*), was also coined.

Tournois (*t.*) coinage of Tours in western France was the dominant silver coinage among about 40 coinages in circulation in France in 1300. *Parisis* (*p.*) coinage was originally Capetian royal coinage in Paris and was also widely employed. The relationship between *Tournois* coins and *Parisis* coins of the same denomination was traditionally four *deniers tournois* (*d. t.*) for five *deniers parisis* (*d. t.*). About the year 1450 the gold florin was worth 25 *s. t.* of silver *Tournois* coinage and about 5/6 of a gold *écu* (30 *s. t.*). Further equivalences for monetary sums are signaled in the text.

Index